IN
VIETNAM

Illustrated with photographs

Atheneum   New York   1985

IN VIETNAM

by Denis J. Hauptly

PHOTO CREDITS

Defense Department 56, 101-104, 137-140
National Archives TP, 54, 55, 57

Library of Congress Cataloging in Publication Data

Hauptly, Denis J.   In Vietnam.

*SUMMARY: Discusses the turbulent history of Vietnam
from the Chinese invasion 2000 years ago through the
United States' involvement during the 1960s.*
*1. Vietnam—History—Juvenile literature.   2. United
States—Foreign relations—Vietnam—Juvenile literature.
3. Vietnam—Foreign relations—United States—Juvenile
literature. 4. Vietnamese Conflict, 1961–1975—United
States—Juvenile literature. [1. Vietnam—History.
2. Vietnamese Conflict, 1961—1975] I. Title.*
DS556.5.H38   1985   959.7   85-7464

TO
Genevieve Elaine Hauptly
John James Hauptly
Sarah Howard Blackwell
AND
Kara Hauptly

Contents

INTRODUCTION xiii

one   An Ancient Land   3

two   From Empire to Colony   17

three   Indochina   29

four   The Indochina War   42

five   A Tale of Two Cities   58

six   A Tale of Two Presidents   72

seven   In Tonkin Gulf   88

eight   Thunder and Lightning   105

nine   Over There   115

ten   1968   124

eleven   Talking Peace   141

twelve   After the War Was Over   157

BIBLIOGRAPHY   167

INDEX   171

ACKNOWLEDGEMENTS

I would like to acknowledge the kind and thoughtful advice of Dr. Henry Fairbanks, Professor Emeritus at St. Michael's College. His comments, especially with regard to the character of President Diem have saved me from error on this as on so many other occasions.

I would also like to thank Peg Murphy who prepared the manuscript with considerable promptness and patience.

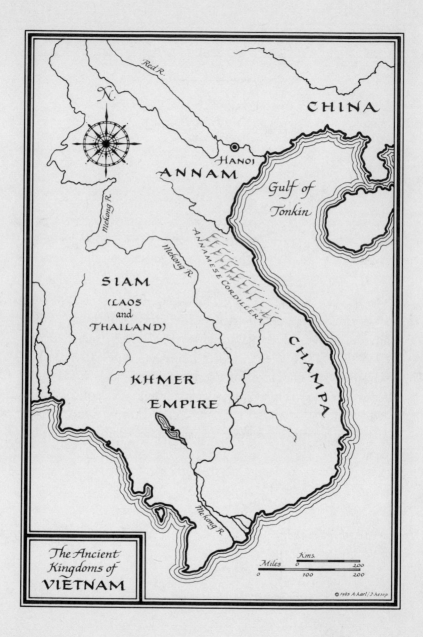

The Ancient
Kingdoms of
VIETNAM

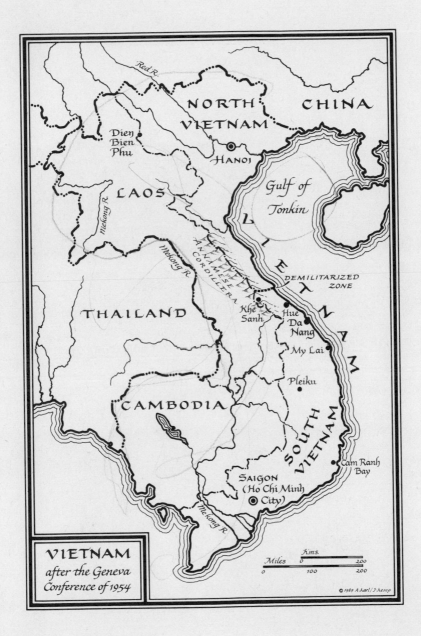

Red R.

NORTH CHINA
VIETNAM

Dien
Bien
Phu

HANOI

Gulf of
Tonkin

LAOS

Mekong R.

ANNAMESE
CORDILLERA

Mekong R.

DEMILITARIZED
ZONE

Khe
Sanh

Hue
Da
Nang

THAILAND

My Lai

Pleiku

CAMBODIA

SOUTH
VIETNAM

Cam Ranh
Bay

SAIGON
(Ho Chi Minh
City)

Mekong R.

VIETNAM
after the Geneva
Conference of 1954

Kms.
Miles   0   200
0   100   200

© 1985 A.Karl/J.Kemp

Introduction

The word "Vietnam" means different things to different people today. To many it means an issue that was the center of attention during eight years of American life. To others, who fought in it, it recalls the friendships and sorrows of combat, or moments of personal bravery or great fear.

In a large sense Vietnam means failure. Whether that was a failure of the American government or a failure of the American people can be argued. In the chapters ahead we will view the war in Southeast Asia from its very beginnings and that may make the debate clearer. One of the first things we will see is that war in Vietnam did not begin with the arrival of American troops or even with the earlier arrival of French troops. War began a century before Christ and continues to this day.

This is important. To see the Vietnam war as ten years of American conflict is to miss its basic character. It is like watching a thirty second report on the evening news. One can learn some facts in that time but one cannot gain understanding. We need to understand Vietnam. We need to know why it happened, as well as how it happened. We need to grasp the nature of the failure in order to draw lessons from it for the future.

The Vietnam War was a complex of events. Like most such events its meaning changes with the viewpoint of the person watching it. On many of the important issues involving the conduct of the war there are at least two different stories of what happened and why it happened. But, even so, this doesn't mean that we can't draw lessons from it.

The assassination of President Kennedy in 1963 is not a very complex event. Yet there are many different stories about how it happened. Some say the deed was done by a lone assassin. Others argue that there must have been two or more persons involved. Even those who hold with the conspiracy view argue about who was involved in it. Some say the Russians planned it. Others say it was the C.I.A. Some think it was Fidel Castro while others favor J. Edgar Hoover or organized crime.

Soon after the event the answers to these questions were very important. As time went by, they became much less so. The question that will affect the world for many years is not how the assassination came about but what came about because of the assassination.

This is also true of Vietnam. What happened and how it happened are still important. Was the president lied to by the military? Did the president lie to the American people? Were the Viet Cong a group seeking freedom for their people or were they part of some international communist plot? The answers to these questions would provide a basis for better ways for America to deal with the world around it in the future, so these questions should not be ignored.

But there are bigger and more important questions, whose answers can be lost if our only worry is on placing blame and finding fault. Why was America in Vietnam? Did it have a good reason? If the reason was good, why did America fail to reach its goal? If the reason was bad, how should large and powerful nations behave in the future?

These are not easy questions and they will not be more than partly answered in this book.

No one would disagree with the idea that we should avoid another involvement like Vietnam, but there would be widespread disagreement as to what "Vietnam" was. When we were very young we all were afraid of "monsters." But if we all were asked to write down what a monster was we would get some pretty different answers. Vampires and werewolves would fill the pages of those who have been frightened by Dracula movies. Trolls and ogres would be described by those who grew up on Grimms' Fairy Tales. Before we can deal with "monsters," we must agree on what a "monster" is. So understanding "Vietnam" is something we must do as well. For just as Vietnam was an important matter for your parents, its unanswered questions may be of great importance to you.

But the war in Vietnam is not simply something to draw lessons from. It is a story too. Indeed, it is the basic story of the second half of the twentieth century. It was a battle between Western machinery and Eastern patience; between two different social systems; between the New World and the Third World; between Catholics and Buddhists; between rich and poor; between colonialism and nationalism; between white and yellow.

And within these battles are countless stories. The stories of presidents in political struggle; the stories of soldiers in war; the story of hometown protests of the actions of the government, in the United States and in Vietnam; the story of government itself and what its purpose should be.

The tale that follows is complicated. In World War II most of the important events took place on the battlefield with thousands of witnesses. In Vietnam they often took place in the president's office in Washington or Ho Chi Minh's office in Vietnam. We know a great deal about what happened in Washington and almost nothing about the thinking in the city of Hanoi in Vietnam. It is difficult to know what really happened, but that makes the task of learning about Vietnam difficult, not hopeless.

There are more useful lessons to be drawn from this conflict than from any other event of this century. That we have to work hard to understand Vietnam doesn't mean that it is not worthwhile to do so.

IN
VIETNAM

ONE

An Ancient Land

Between the Philippines and India there is an odd-looking part of Asia that seems to be hanging from China. It is called Indochina and the nations of Thailand, Laos, Cambodia and Vietnam are found there. It is three times the size of California with five times the number of people as that state.

Along the eastern coast of Indochina, on the South China Sea, is the land we now know as Vietnam. Round at the north, narrowing to a thin mountain range in the center and widening and curving in the south, it looks like the long poles that Asian farmers carry on their shoulders with a rice basket on each end.

That picture is a good one, for the northern bowl contains the rich Red River valley and the southern bowl contains the rice-growing Mekong River delta. Down the center runs the Annamese Cordillera, a rugged range of mountains running from the western borders almost to the sea on the east. It is like an hour glass with its center blocked.

Vietnam's story as a nation begins around 2000 B.C.— or so an ancient story has it. A prince named Lac-Long-Quan was said to have married a fairy called Au-Co. Au-Co is said to have laid one hundred eggs. These hatched into sons and half went north into China while the other half stayed and founded Vietnam.

The real story, of course, is not so fanciful. In the fourth century before Christ, the kingdom of the Viet people in southern China was attacked by invaders and fell. Its people fled south, settling in the Red River delta near the city we now call Hanoi. They called their new home Nam Viet, and China hung over it like a dark and dangerous cloud.

In 111 B.C., the cloud burst and the Chinese moved south. The Chinese had recently thrown out foreign invaders who had been troubling them for a century. Freedom from trouble at home gave them a new strength, and they sought to expand their territory. The new nation was easily captured and became the Chinese province of Giao Chi. It remained a captive for one thousand years. (The United States has been an independent country for only two hundred years.) The province extended as far south as the city of Hue (pronounced "Hway") which is near the center of the narrow waist of modern Vietnam.

This long period of captivity had two important re-

sults. First, to the Viet people, the Chinese were the
enemy, the feared and fearful force always nearby. But
also, the Chinese had a strong influence over the Vietnamese. Chinese culture, religion, language, and desires
were felt in the province for ten centuries and the impact
of those years would not quickly pass away.

But China was like an elephant. It was powerful, yet
so large that its size sometimes worked against it. The
small province rebelled again and again against Chinese
rule, even though its enemy was many times stronger
than it.

The first of these rebellions took place in 40 A.D. when
the Trung sisters, Trung Trac and Trung Nhi, took control of the province and established themselves as joint
queens. Their reign was short-lived because the Chinese
counterattacked and took control again.

The Chinese were alarmed by the rebellion and sought
to strengthen their control of the province through the
commune system. Under this program the province was
broken up into small villages with from five to fifty
families in each. Each village was designed to operate by
itself without outside help. The system discouraged the
people of Nam Viet from working together to throw
out the Chinese. They were like a football team that
played without a huddle. If they could not plan together,
they could not work together. If they could not work
together, they could not overcome the Chinese. The commune system also established the village as the basic
structure in the province, a fact that would be important
for centuries to come.

The Chinese brought something else that would be

important for a long time, too. In 188 A.D., the Chinese
brought the Buddhist religion to the southern province.

Buddhism was founded around 528 B.C. by Siddhartha
Gautama, better known today as the Buddha or "the
enlightened one." Siddhartha was the son of the ruler of
a small country in northern India. He was raised in a
wealthy household and protected from any knowledge
of the troubles of the world. As an adult, of course, he
discovered that there was much unhappiness around him.
The knowledge shocked him, and he abandoned his
family and wealth to seek understanding.

For six years he studied with various holy men, but
did not find the knowledge he was seeking. As a final
effort he vowed to sit beneath a tree (now known as the
Bo Tree) until he understood the purpose of life. After
seven weeks he arose with what he felt was a new and
clearer way of looking at things. He spent the next forty-
five years of his life preaching and practicing what he
had learned.

Buddha taught by preaching, not by writing. It was
centuries before his ideas were written down, and by
that time there was some disagreement as to what the
Buddha had taught. Those differences remain today, and
so it is not possible to say what Buddhism teaches, because
it teaches many different things depending on the branch
of Buddhism.

But if there is one thing that Buddhists generally believe, it is that pain and sorrow are part of our lives and
must simply be accepted. It is better to expect nothing
than to expect happiness. The true Buddhist believes in
the value of self-denial, giving up all worldly goods and

seeking to relieve the troubles of others. Once selfishness is removed from a person, the Buddhist believes that he or she will reach a state of complete peace called "nirvana."

This does not mean that all Buddhists at all times act in this ideal manner. Just as Christians do not always turn the other cheek or love their neighbor, Buddhism has a group of beliefs that its believers often find hard to live up to. But the ideas of patient acceptance of fate and sacrifice are very important in cultures that are influenced by Buddhism.

Despite the Chinese commune system and the peaceful influence of Buddhism, revolts against Chinese rule continued, though the rebellions were often centuries apart. A woman named Trieu Au led the next one in 248 A.D.; Ly Bon tried in 542; Ly Xuan in 589, and Ly Phat Tu in 602. All efforts failed.

They must have had some effect on the Chinese though, because in 679, they decided to grant Giao Chi a limited form of self-government. The province was renamed Annam. This was during the Chinese T'ang Dynasty, a period when China was growing quickly, ruling from Korea to India. It was also one of the great periods in Chinese history. The huge territory China controlled and the great culture it developed gave the Chinese enough security to be willing to allow their provinces more freedom.

The T'Ang Dynasty ended in 906 and was followed by more than fifty years of division in which local lords were more powerful than any central government in China. During this time China divided into seven kingdoms, and five separate dynasties attempted to rule the nation. The people of Annam took advantage of this division in China and under the military leadership of Ngo-Quyan, a local governor, they defeated the Chinese at the battle of Bach Dang and became once more a free nation.

The new nation was called Dai Co Viet, which means the Great Viet State. Established in 968 under Dinh Bo Liuh, it was a feudal society—one with peasants tied to the land and local lords owing allegiance to a national emperor.

Once free of Chinese rule the Viet people turned their attention to the south. They were very much aware of the fact that while China might be weak today, it could be very strong tomorrow. New territory and new people could give the Viet the strength needed to hold off their ancient enemy.

The land south of the Annamese Cordillera was then known as the Kingdom of Champa, which included most of what is now the southern part of Vietnam except for the Mekong Delta area. By 1069, the Viets had taken control of much of Champa, though a final victory was not to come until 1471.

The Viet march to the south is an idea in this story until the very end. Like Buddhism and the relations between Vietnam and China, it is an ancient root which, if kept in mind, makes the events of modern days easier to understand.

Look at the map of Indochina. Notice the border between Vietnam and Cambodia. At the northern end, where Laos, Cambodia and Vietnam join together, the border makes sense. At this point the border follows the foothills of the central mountain range. To the east are mountains and Vietnam. To the west are plains and Cambodia.

In the time before surveyors and border stations and artificial markers such as highways, natural things like mountain ranges and rivers were the borders between nations because they were visible and not subject to much dispute. Also, before planes and large boats were common, such natural borders were easy to defend since they were so difficult for large numbers of people to cross at one time.

But if we follow the Cambodian-Vietnamese border down farther, we find a different situation. As we reach a point of the border just above Ho Chi Minh City, we have reached the end of the mountains and have entered the Mekong River valley—a large and fertile plain that ends in the South China Sea but begins in the heart of Cambodia. Not only is there not a natural border here, but there is the river itself providing both easy transportation and much-needed fertile land. Instead of being a barrier, it was a magnet, pulling people in search of rich farmland to it.

If you were to fly over Indochina and know nothing of its present borders, you might decide that the Mekong Valley from the sea to the Laotian border (where the mountains begin again) was part of one nation. And, in the tenth century, it *was* all part of Cambodia. But once the Viets reached the edges of this territory, they saw it as part of their future. This was not unlike what happened in America in the days of the pioneers. Once they reached the Great Plains of America's Midwest, they saw a land they believed to be their own. They had worked very hard to reach those plains. They had crossed the ocean, pushed aside the Indians, and cut roads through the mountains. The new land was theirs; it was their destiny.

The Viets felt their destiny was to the south and west. This thousand-year-old desire of the Vietnamese people to move up the valley represents another basic fact that was to bear fruit centuries later.

But while the Viets were looking toward Cambodia, someone else was looking at them. Early in the thirteenth century the Mongol leader Genghis Khan began to move from his small central Asia base to create one of the largest empires of all time. Striking in every direction, Genghis Khan's forces soon took Europe as far west as Poland, much of Russia to the north, as well as the northern half of China. His death in 1227 slowed the Mongol expansion for a while, but his sons firmed up the Mongol rule in the new territories and his grandsons began to spread the empire farther. Among these grandsons was Kublai Khan, who would become a powerful force. But not too powerful for the Vietnamese.

Between 1268 and 1284, Kublai Khan completed the Mongol invasion of China. He became the Emperor Shis-Tsu, the founder of the Yuan Dynasty, and turned his attention to Indochina. Three times he invaded and three times he was beaten, the last time by the great Viet general Tran Hung Dao. Tran met five hundred thousand Mongols with two hundred thousand Viets and defeated the invaders. His military exploits remain legendary in Vietnam to this day.

The Mongols were forced from China itself in 1398 by a fighting Buddhist monk (a very odd thing) named Chu Yuan-Chang. This new Chinese regime was greatly concerned about the security of its borders. In the north they expanded the Great Wall of China and in the south they moved again into the land they called Annam. From 1406 to 1428 it was once again a Chinese province, but the Chinese rule was never firm.

The leader of the Viet opposition was Le Loi, a wealthy landowner. He knew that an open battle with the Chinese was useless. There were too many Chinese and they had the use of gunpowder. Instead of fighting major battles, he used small groups of soldiers who would attack a Chinese fort and disappear quickly. After ten years of struggle, the Chinese were worn down and left. Le Loi established the Le dynasty which ruled Vietnam for three hundred and fifty years. Vietnam, which was still largely the northern half of the modern nation, was secure from Chinese rule—if not from Chinese influence.

But no sooner had the Vietnamese expelled the Chinese than a new group of foreigners began to make their presence felt.

In 1487, a Portuguese sailor named Bartholomew Diaz achieved an ancient goal when he rounded the Cape of Good Hope at the southern tip of Africa. Once this feat had been accomplished, it was only a matter of time before the great Portuguese sailors reached their main goal —India. Vasco da Gama landed there in 1497, and the riches of India were opened to Portuguese trade.

The Portuguese kept their route a secret, because they wanted all the riches of Asia for themselves. They sought to increase their hold over Asian sea trade by traveling

to China and Japan. By the early 1500s they had opened
trade to both countries. They could not travel these seas
for long, though, without coming to Vietnam. Its position on the South China Sea was an impotrant one and
the fertile Red River region was a choice place to trade.
This discovery finally took place in 1535, when the
Portuguese captain Antonio de Faria dropped anchor in
Da Nang Bay near Hue.

It would be pleasant to say that these first encounters
with Europeans were good for both sides. It would be
pleasant, but untrue. A large part of the early European
trade involved firearms. This trade was a rich one, for the
Vietnamese, while free from outside troubles for the
first time in centuries, were now involved in a long and
bitter conflict among themselves. The Le dynasty had
grown weak and the real power in the nation was held
by two families. The Trinh held sway in the north and
the Nguyen in the south, in what had been the kingdom
of Champa. Both sides felt that they were the true leaders
of the Vietnamese people.

On paper at least the struggle should have been one-
sided. The northern part of Vietnam was strong, with
a stable government and a large number of people. The
south had a much smaller population and had not yet
fully established its government.

But the population of the north worked against it too.
There was not enough land to feed the people, and much
of that land was controlled by rich landowners. The
people were hungry and angry. Many moved to the south
where land was available and government was not as
strict. The Trinh in the north had very weak support

from their large population, while the Nguyen had strong support from their smaller population.

The Trinh were backed by the Dutch, who had followed the Portuguese to Asia, and the Nguyen were backed by the Portuguese. The civil war continued until a truce in 1673. By that time the Nguyen felt safe enough on their northern border to turn south and continue their expansion. The Mekong Delta was then part of Cambodia, but by 1700 it had become part of the still-divided Vietnam.

Between 1650 and 1770, the Nguyen invaded Cambodia eleven times. They never succeeded in taking it entirely, but each attack expanded Vietnamese influence in the area.

Despite the southern expansion and the military successes of the Nguyen, Vietnam was a troubled land. It was still basically a feudal society divided into small, independent regions each headed by a feudal lord. Its economy was divided as well. Each village was designed to produce what it needed and the needs were few.

A feeling of nationhood usually has some economic root. Where one region produces food and another coal, and the ties of language and religion are strong, a bond develops that often leads to national unity. The independence of the Vietnamese villages worked against national unity, but at the same time the villages provided another strength.

The village life was communal. The fields were held in common and worked in common. In each of the villages the bonds of family were strong. So the village represented a powerful force that neither the decaying Le dynasty, which still ruled the nation in name, nor the Trinh or Nguyen families had learned to use.

In 1772, though, three brothers from the village of Tay Son rose against the leaders of Vietnam. Taking their name from their village, the Tay Son brothers led the last of the dozens of peasant revolts that had shaken the nation for a hundred years.

They started in the south, and in 1777, while American revolutionaries were suffering the cold winter of Valley Forge, they overthrew the Nguyen family in the south. Nine years later they had conquered the Trinh family and had removed the last of the Le dynasty from the throne. For the first time in two centuries Vietnam was one nation again. Really it was a new and much more powerful nation, for the earlier expansion into the Mekong Delta that took place during the Trinh-Nguyen division increased the country to its present borders.

Other changes had taken place too. The Europeans, who had brought firearms into the struggle, had brought a more gentle force as well—Christianity.

This was the age of exploration in Europe, which took place at the same time as the religious Reformation. To Catholics and Protestants alike this was a difficult period. They were changing their ideas about the geographic world at the same time as they were changing their views on spiritual life. It is not surprising that the explorers felt that their travels and their contacts with new nations were part of the great spiritual battle that divided the European nations.

The Portuguese and Spanish explorers and merchants who came to Vietnam brought priests with them. It was important to them that part of their search for riches also involved a search for souls. As time went by, though, the largest numbers of missionary priests came from France. Because many converts to Christianity were members of the most powerful families, the French grew to have more influence than other European countries in Vietnam.

At the dawn of the nineteenth century, Vietnam was united as a nation and as a government, but deeply divided in other ways. Rich and poor, north and south, Buddhist and Catholic are just the clearest groups into which the Vietnamese could be placed. In the new nation there were many people other than the Viets. And supporters of the Le dynasty or the Trinh and Nguyen families still had some power.

The unity of Vietnam then was a very fragile thing, and the increasing interest of the Europeans in Asia was a danger to that unity and to the independence that brought it about.

The Age of Exploration was turning into the Age of Imperialism. The colonies of the New World, which had once supplied great wealth to the nations of Europe, were breaking free from their homelands. The European powers were turning to Africa and Asia as they lost their Western sources of supplies and trade. But the Europeans were no longer content just to trade; they wanted to gain control in the East to make up for their lost colonies in the West. With superior weapons and with political unity they looked about for likely lands. Vietnam was one of those lands.

TWO

From Empire To Colony

The Tay Son brothers had reunited Vietnam under their control, but it was still not really a nation. No one force was powerful enough to end the divisions. But the Nguyen family found an ally that made it very powerful indeed. The ally was France.

As we know, the French had long been interested in Vietnam both as a trading center and as a place for missionary work. In 1787, a new wave of French missionaries had come to Vietnam from India, and they believed that if they had more say in the government of Vietnam their religious work would become easier.

The Catholic Church was very powerful in France in those days, which were just before the French Revolution, and the missionaries were able to supply French weapons to the Nguyen faction. Then, when the revolution came in France, that nation was divided and was unable to aid the missionaries' efforts. But by 1802, Napoleon had mastered and quieted France and the missionaries were again able to get artillery for their friends.

With this help the Nguyens defeated the Trinhs, and Gia Long became emperor of all of Vietnam. The new emperor adopted the Chinese mandarin system to govern the nation. The mandarins were local administrators. Anyone could become a mandarin by passing a test. This testing system had some funny results. It meant, first, that even the poorest of the poor could move into a position of power, wealth and influence. But the test was based on knowledge of the past, not ideas about the future, so those who best knew the past were the ones who moved up in the world. Such people were not likely to value great social change. While they themselves moved upward in society, they had no interest in making changes in the basic ways of that society. To them, the old ways were always the best ways. The mandarin system was then both very democratic and open and at the same time very rigid and conservative.

But living in the past was the one thing the Vietnamese could not afford to do at that point in their history. The world around them was changing and was closing in on them. England, Portugal, Spain and the Netherlands were opening huge colonial empires in Asia and profiting handsomely from those empires.

In order to meet this new challenge, Vietnam had to create a sense of nationhood among all its people and had to form a powerful military to stop the French and others from trying to move in. The military situation was nearly hopeless. While Vietnam had a large population, it had no tradition of a professional military. When problems that needed military answers came up, generals would be appointed and peasants called into the ranks of the army. As soon as the crisis passed, everyone went back to whatever they had been doing beforehand. Such a system might work well enough when the only problem was a local rebellion involving people who knew as little about fighting as the national army, but it had no chance at all against the experienced forces of a nation like France.

The chief obstacle to the sense of national unity was the land system. The majority of the Vietnamese were poor peasants who worked fields owned by rich landowners for a small portion of the crop. They had no interest in the nation or its rulers. If the French came and took over, they would be working for the French not the local mandarin. Their life was their village not their nation.

Gia Long made some efforts to change this. He ordered large landholdings broken up, but these orders were often not followed by the mandarins, and the emperor had no real power to force his will upon them. Some days even emperors must find it hard to get up in the morning and go to work.

Gia Long also wanted to increase the size of Vietnam, and thus provide more land for the people. In 1803, he began a new effort to take control of Cambodia. For two hundred years the Cambodian people had fought off the Vietnamese and the Thais. This time they would lose a final battle. By 1834, most of modern Cambodia was under Vietnamese rule. The Cambodians never forgave the Vietnamese for this conquest, and their hatred of the Vietnamese was to bear bitter fruit more than a century later.

The French Catholic missionaries in Vietnam were disappointed by Gia Long. They felt that their help in setting up his regime entitled them to some support from the government. Gia Long and the emperors who followed him felt differently. To them the presence of the French missionaries was not simply a religious matter but, instead, was an attempt at French control, a control that would mean the end of Vietnamese independence.

Even if the missionaries were not trying to take control of the Vietnam government, their presence spelled a danger. Europeans and Asians represent very different ways of life and values. The missionaries wanted their converts to choose values similar to their own, and there was not enough room in Vietnam for two so different cultures. Europe was increasingly industrial and democratic. Asia remained a farming society, and its leaders were chosen by the few, not the many.

In 1825, the Vietnamese began to persecute Christians in the nation. It is important to remember that the persecution was not intended to put an end to the Christian religion in Vietnam. It was directed at the French missionaries, who were seen as, and in many ways were, a part of the French government. They were close to the leaders of the French government and many of their actions were designed to increase their government's hold on Vietnam. Church and state were not separate.

In persecuting Christians, the Vietnamese were attempting to protect their society from being drowned by European society. This persecution was not praiseworthy, but the political activities of the missionaries opened the door to its use.

There followed a long time in which the missionaries and their followers were first persecuted and then left alone. The persecution was more a matter of law than of fact, but the missionaries often felt that they had to flee Vietnam for safety in other nations. Some of them were jailed, although they were quickly released.

In all of this time, the French government itself interfered little, for France was having problems of its own. The great Napoleon was defeated and sent into exile. He returned in triumph with a new army only to be defeated again at Waterloo. He was replaced by a king from the family he had helped throw out, but the king too lasted only a short time. He was followed by a new Emperor Napoleon, a relative of the first. France had little time or money for involvement in far-off Asia. These facts may have made the Vietnamese feel safe when they really were not.

By 1842, the French game of "king of the mountain" seemed to have ended, and they were in a colonial mood again. A French fleet was sent to Asia to look into trading opportunities with China. While there, they learned that the Vietnamese had imprisoned a French bishop. The fleet sailed for Vietnam where it met a Vietnamese fleet —which it promptly sank. The bishop was released and the fleet took control of the southern city of Saigon for a short time.

But the peace in France had ended as quickly as it had

come. The Revolution of 1848 delayed any efforts to take advantage of the weakness of the Vietnamese.

Even if all had been quiet at home, the French may not have moved on Vietnam for some time. The French leaders did not agree about the wisdom of taking Asian colonies. If you have a colony, and it is a good colony, other nations might like to have it as well. After all, if you felt that Vietnam was worth taking, England might think it was worth taking from you. That means you have to be ready to fight off whatever size army England might send. To supply and defend a colony thousands of miles from home requires enormous resources that many felt would better be used in Europe. And a colony in Vietnam did not promise a quick profit. It was a farming nation and the farming methods were poor. While Vietnam could be a source of wealth, for the moment it was just a poor country.

In fact, the main reason to take control in Vietnam was to set up a trading route to China. To be successful, though, such a route needed to be on water, since products are cheaper to move on water than on land. Land travel is slow and, at that time, required food for the animals who pulled the wagons as well as good roads to move them on. River travel was faster, boats could be as large as the river could carry, and no animals had to be fed. But the French were not sure that there was a river that ran from Vietnam to China.

By 1857, the French government under Louis Napoleon was listening to the pleas of the missionaries and the business people for a Vietnamese colony. The first step was a careful one. In November, a French fleet was sent to the Vietnamese port of Tourane. The port was taken. And although the missionaries had told the French that such an action would spark a rebellion by Vietnamese Catholics, the rebellion did not take place. The French moved forward to Saigon, the principal city of the Mekong River area. Saigon fell to the French in February of 1859.

But all was not well with the French. They had the troops and they had the weapons, but they could not control the weather and the weather is a very tough opponent.

If you have ever been to the ocean in summertime, you probably have noticed that it is cooler at the beach than it is in other places. You may also have noticed that a wind blows straight in from the ocean across the beach. If you were to go to the same beach on a winter's day you would probably find the wind blowing from the land into the sea.

These seasonal winds in Asia are known as monsoons, and they are caused by the difference between the temperature of the land and the temperature of the water. Hot air and cold air push against each other. The motion of the air causes winds. The greater the difference in temperature, the stronger the winds. Each year in the spring the monsoon begins to blow from the ocean across Southeast Asia. As it passes over the ocean it picks up water and brings it across the land. Once over the land, the water is released in the form of rain that pours from the sky for months on end.

The monsoon today makes military operations in Southeast Asia very difficult. In 1860 it made them impossible. There were no tanks or other special machinery to move through the mud and water. So the French were bogged down for much of the year. And while they were bogged down, they had the opportunity to encounter tropical diseases that they had not met in France.

This combination of weather and disease badly hurt the French forces, and they could only have been saved by fresh troops from France. But no such help came because the French were involved in a war with Austria. The French commanders had no choice but to withdraw from Tourane in 1860 and move all of their troops into the Saigon area.

The next year some new French troops came, and the French expanded their area of control around Saigon. By 1862, the French had taken control of a large area in the Mekong River delta, but they were running into trouble once more.

Even with the new help the French troops were spread thin. That made them easy to attack by small groups of guerrillas ("guerrillas" are soldiers who are not in uniform and who drift back into the crowd after they fight. The Minutemen in the Revolutionary War were guerrilllas.) The French were looking for a way out of their dilemma. The Vietnamese gave them one. Trouble in North Vietnam from Vietnamese who opposed the government made it necessary for the emperor to divide his already weak forces between two battle areas.

The emperor was more worried about the internal rebellions than the French. His feeling was that if the rebellions were first put down, he could turn his whole military force against the French and both problems would end. In order to do this he needed to buy time with the French, and the best way to do that, he thought, was to officially give up what he had already lost—the Saigon region.

In June of 1862, the emperor agreed to French control of that area and turned his attention to the north. If he felt that the French would be happy with what they had, though, he was quite wrong.

Over the next five years the French continued to expand their area of control in the South. By 1867, they controlled not only the entire Mekong River delta in Vietnam, but also they had managed to so threaten the Cambodians that that nation allowed France to establish a protectorate over it. In its best sense, a "protectorate" is an agreement between two free nations in which the stronger nation says that it will look out for the welfare of the weaker one. In the worst sense, it is the takeover of the weaker nation by the stronger without the need to fight for the result. France's protectorate over Cambodia was nearer to the worst type, though the Cambodians had long lived in fear of both the Vietnamese and the Thais, and they knew that they needed all the protection that they could get.

The French referred to their conquests in the southern part of Indochina as "Cochinchina" (meaning "Southern China"). While the Vietnamese did not yet accept it, this large and fertile area was now a province of France. And it seemed for a while that the French were satisfied with what they had. Actually they were not.

While the missionaries and traders continued to push for a French takeover of all of Vietnam, the French government was not sure that it wanted to commit the forces needed to do that. It was still very uncertain that any money could be made in Vietnam, and a river route to China had not been discovered. French explorers had traveled up the Mekong River only to find that large ships could not go far up its shallow waters, and besides, it headed away from China. In the early 1870s, though, a French adventurer named Dupuis took a secret trip up the Red River in northern Vietnam and found the long-desired trade route.

He worked out a plot with French officials in Saigon, and in 1873 seized and held part of the northern city of Hanoi. The French in Saigon then told Emperor Tu Duc that they would send troops to help rid the city of this Frenchman. These troops, led by the young François Garnier, went instead to help Dupuis. Within a few months Garnier's troops had taken control of a large part of northern Vietnam. Garnier called himself the Great French Mandarin. While the title was certainly grand, it did Garnier little good, because he was killed in battle by the end of the year.

The whole effort of Dupuis and Garnier had been carried out without permission from the French government. When Paris heard what had gone on, the government became greatly concerned about having its troops tied down in Vietnam at a time when Europe was once more at war. French forces were ordered to withdraw from northern Vietnam. In exchange the emperor yielded all control over the south. France had half of Vietnam.

The war in Europe was the Franco-Prussian War. In it the French forces were easily defeated by the Prussians of Germany. It was many years before the French economy and military regained its strength. Not until the early 1880s was France prepared for foreign conquest, and by then it had very strong reasons to gain colonies.

The Industrial Revolution was sweeping through the Western world. The new machinery was capable of producing many times the amount of goods that had been made by hand only a few years before. It was wonderful, of course, to be able to produce huge amounts of goods, but the production of goods is of no value unless one can sell them. There were no buyers in Europe, because everyone else was making the same goods. The answer to this problem was to seek new markets in areas not yet touched by the Industrial Revolution. Again French thoughts turned toward Vietnam.

With the blessings of the French government six hundred troops under the direction of Captain Henri Rivière moved from Saigon to Hanoi in 1882. The city was quickly taken, though Rivière died in battle. More French troops and naval forces followed. Emperor Tu Duc died in July of 1883, and in the confusion that followed his death, Vietnamese resistance, which had always been weak, collapsed entirely. On August 25, 1883, the Vietnamese government agreed to the Treaty of Protectorate giving the French control of the nation. Vietnamese independence was once more at an end.

The French moved swiftly to establish their authority over Vietnam. One of their first acts was to drop the word "Vietnam" itself. The southern area retained the name of Cochinchina and was made a colony of France. The northern portion was called Tonkin, and the French established it as a protectorate. The mountainous central region was called Annam and the new emperor was in charge there, or at least that was the idea.

The French also established strong central governments, which reduced the role and influence of the local mandarins. They ended the testing program that had been the road to success for many peasants. They even took away the common lands, which had been the peasants' main source of income, and turned them into large plantations on which the peasants were simply hired farmers.

These changes were greater in Cochinchina because the French had been there longer and because their rule over the colony was stronger than their rule over the other parts of the nation. There were always differences between the north and the south. Under French rule they grew wider.

The people of Vietnam had not really supported the emperor against the French. They had little love for their national government. But neither did they welcome the French when they took over. The poverty, which they had previously blamed on the mandarins, they now blamed on the French. For three years they strongly opposed French rule, and in this they were aided by the Chinese, who had no desire to have a strong European power at their doorstep.

But by 1887 the French were in control. In that year they formed the Indochinese Union, an organization of the French-controlled parts of Indochina, including Cambodia. In 1893, the French took over Laos, which gave them complete control of the Mekong River. Laos too became part of the Indochinese Union.

Not all of the Vietnamese accepted French rule, but

by the beginning of the twentieth century, peace and the French ruled in Southeast Asia. For the next fifty years this ancient land would be known as French Indochina, and the seeds of the next phase in Vietnamese history would be sown by young Vietnamese educated in French schools and looking forward to a free Vietnam that they had never known. How those seeds grew and the strange paths that the future leaders of Vietnam followed is a complex story. In its twists and turns are the causes of French defeat in Vietnam and the American involvement in a place that few Americans had even heard of in the early 1900s.

THREE

Indochina

The years of French colo-
nial rule began with an
effort at modernizing Vietnam. The paths of commerce
were built: roads, bridges, railroads and harbors. But the
commerce that traveled those paths was French commerce. Taking Indochina had cost the French a lot of
money, and they meant to get their money back quickly.

They did this in three ways. First, they took the wealth
of Vietnam: the metals and the timber were removed
and the rice harvested and taken back to France. Second,
they took over the sale of important goods. Salt, alcohol
and other products were made the subject of a French
monopoly. If a Vietnamese peasant needed to buy Vietnamese salt he had to buy it from the French at the price
that the French set. This was an important matter. There

were no refrigerators in Vietnam. If you wanted to keep the fish you caught one day to eat at a later time, you needed salt to preserve it. Control of salt was as much a power over the Vietnamese as control of electricity would be over an American.

Third, if the Vietnamese wanted to buy products from another country, those products were generally brought in from France. More than half of all goods brought into Vietnam came from France, and the buyer had to pay a tariff or tax for the privilege.

It is not that the French rule did not improve the economy. It did. But the benefits of those improvements went mostly to the French and to large Vietnamese landowners. The French had turned around the plan to turn land over to the peasants. By 1914, nearly half of the land in Vietnam was owned by only two percent of the people. More than half the people owned no land at all.

In modern western society numbers like these would not be very important. Most people in modern Europe or America live in cities and work in factories or offices. Owning land is important to them, but their lives do not depend on it. But Vietnam was and is a rural and agricultural society. One who owned no land was one who had to lead a life of poverty from which there was no escape.

And an awful poverty it was. Harvests were poor in those early years of French rule and even landowners went hungry. There were no schools for average people and almost no medical care. There was one doctor for every thirty-eight thousand Vietnamese, as compared to one for every thirty-two hundred in the Philippines at the same time.

Not all Frenchmen ignored the plight of the Vietnamese people. One early governor-general (the title given to the French colonial leader), Paul Beau, tried to open opportunities for education and some role in the government to the Vietnamese. But this program came too late to make a real difference and its title, "the moral conquest," suggests that its real goal was not to benefit the Vietnamese but to secure control of the colony by capturing the souls of the population. When we later talk about the American involvement in Vietnam, we will see similar names for nonmilitary programs such as "pacification" and "winning the hearts and minds of the Vietnamese."

This form of colonial rule was bound to have its results. Even before World War I began in 1914, Vietnamese intellectuals began to form secret nationalist groups. The nationalist movement in Vietnam lies at the very heart of much that will follow. But it is not easy to understand, in part because it was so deeply affected by things that happened in other countries, and in part because the very word "nationalism" meant many different things to many different people.

This last point is easier to explain. As we have already seen, Vietnam had no real political tradition. In the United States, people have gotten used to the idea of an elected Congress and president and of judges who are appointed for life. In Great Britain the tradition of Parliamentary rule and a king or queen goes back for hundreds of years.

In those nations those systems are accepted and honored. Americans would laugh at the idea of a queen, though most would happily agree that the British system works quite well. The British, on the other hand, find American presidential politics a strange way to select leaders. But, again, they probably feel that if Americans are happy with it that then they have no reason to complain.

Our political traditions are sacred in a sense, and we would not change them. If some other tradition was imposed upon us, we would seek not merely to be rid of it but to return to the old system.

Many Vietnamese wanted to be rid of the new French system, but they had little to go back to. There had been and still was an emperor. But in a country where the village is more important than the nation, national government, be it an emperor or anything else, has little meaning. Also, as we have seen, the emperor rarely ruled more than a small part of the country at a time.

What kind of government would the new nation of Vietnam have? Would it return to the full power of the emperor? Would it be a democracy? Would it be a "dictatorship of the proletariat" as Karl Marx had been calling for in his new theory of communism?

These questions divided the Vietnamese as much as any previous questions had divided them. The divided nationalist movement was a very weak thing at first, but it drew strength from three events in the early part of the twentieth century: the Russo-Japanese War, the Chinese Revolution, and World War I. Some years later a similar event—World War II—was to provide the movement with the chance it needed to succeed.

But let us look at these first three struggles in foreign lands and see how they contributed to the events that were to follow.

For hundreds of years the nations of Europe had been taking control of parts of Asia. By 1900, the European control was nearly complete. Only China and Japan of the major Asian nations were independent, and China was only barely so since the nations of Europe as well as the United States had forced the Chinese to allow them special trading rights and privileges. For a time, the Americans even had courts and post offices in China.

The Westerners believed in, and many Asian people seemed to accept, the concept of Western superiority. Certainly this was true in one sense. The Industrial Revolution had provided the Western world with superior arms and means of transportation. These, in turn, made the nations of Asia easy prey for Western colonial plans. They could not strike back at Europe because they had no real navies and they could not defend their own lands against Europe's artillery.

But Japan was different. It was extremely well organized as a nation. Moreover, once Japan opened contact with the West, it lost little time in catching up with industrial development. But Japan was a nation isolated from others both by the water that surrounded it and by choice. The Western world was not fully aware of the powerful nation that was developing off the coast of China.

During the late 1800s the Russians began to ease their way into Chinese territory. By 1904, they controlled most of the area surrounding the then-Japanese province of Korea. The Japanese felt that a move on Korea was next and that if that happened the Russians would use Korea as a jumping-off place for the invasion of Japan itself. The Japanese went to war to stop this.

The results shocked the world, for the Japanese did not just defeat the Russians, they humiliated them in a very short time and even forced the Russians to give up some of their territory to Japan.

The Russo-Japanese War destroyed the idea of Western superiority. It also caused many Asians to see the Japanese as a friend against Western imperialism.

The second event, the Chinese Revolution, took place in 1911, under the leadership of Dr. Sun Yat-sen. His National People's Party—the Kuomintang—sought to free China from control by foreign nations and to establish a program of social justice with a democratic government. With the help of some army officials, Sun was able to overthrow the emperor, but the leaders of many of the provinces would not accept his rule, and the revolution was really more of a long civil war. Nonetheless, for a number of years, China became a place where Vietnamese nationalists could seek safety and where many of them adopted the democratic principles of the Kuomintang.

World War I was fought far away from Vietnam, of course. But it had very important effects there. More than one hundred thousand Vietnamese were moved to Europe to fight on the French side. They found a society that was, to them, wealthy even in the midst of war. They found peasants who owned their own land and could make a living out of it. They found a democracy where even peasants had a vote. They learned that progress was possible.

Without that simple idea there may have been no

real nationalist movement in Vietnam. After all, there was no benefit to the large number of peasants in Vietnam to fight and die for the nationalist cause if it only meant that leadership would change from the French, who were cheating them, to their own countrymen, who would do the same. If, on the other hand, a revolution offered them the promise of a better life for themselves and their children, then it might be worthwhile after all. The war also provided what seemed to be a good opportunity to strike while the French were weak and distracted.

There had been several nationalist leaders and movements before World War I. Listing them all would only show that the movement was divided and weak. In 1916, though, in the midst of World War I, a new nationalist effort was mounted by educated government officials in support of the eighteen-year-old emperor, Duy Ton. This effort was better organized and more broadly based than the previous nationalist revolts had been, but its strategy involved open rebellion against French troops with their superior arms and training. And, while the French were quite busy fighting the Germans in Europe, their weapons and skills were still such that they had little trouble with the Vietnamese. The 1916 rebellion failed and hundreds of Vietnamese were executed.* Many more were sent into exile, including Emperor Duy Ton. In his place the French elevated Khai Dinh to the throne.

Of course, not all of the educated Vietnamese opposed

---

* In 1916, the Irish tried to throw the British out of their country, too. They also felt that World War I gave them a chance to strike while their rulers were weak. They failed to do so. In 1917, Russian revolutionaries began their civil war for the same reason. The Russians were successful, though.

the French colonial rule. Many of them found that by cooperating with the French they could make substantial profits for themselves. Similarly, some wealthy Vietnamese, either hoping to protect their positions through allying themselves with the French or hoping to provide their families with a better education than was available in Vietnam, sent their children to France to study. Many of these children returned as young adults with revolutionary attitudes. Just like the soldiers in World War I, they saw things in France that they wanted for their own people, and they felt that these things would never come to Vietnam so long as the French ruled the nation.

In this they were correct, for while some governors-general sought to liberalize colonial rule and to allow Vietnamese participation in the government of the colony, their efforts along this path were not very significant. For the most part they involved allowing the Vietnamese to form political parties such as the Constitutionalist Party, which sought to influence but not really end French colonial rule.

The French did not allow true nationalists to start political parties, but this did not stop them from doing so. One could spend many chapters telling the story of these organizations and their leaders. But for our purposes we can look to those founded by Ho Chi Minh.

Ho was born in the northern part of Vietnam in the year 1890. The name he is best known by is simply the last of a series of names he took during his lifetime, changing it to express some political thought (as when he called himself Nguyen Ai Fuocor "Nguyen the Patriot") or to avoid capture by the French.

He left Vietnam in 1911 and traveled throughout

Asia and Europe, finally settling in Paris in 1919. Many Vietnamese were in Paris at the end of World War I, and Ho preached a national revolution to them and edited the newspaper *Le Paria*. While Ho was certainly a nationalist at this time, it is difficult to say what sort of nation he envisioned. Certainly his own ideas were changing rapidly.

At first he joined the Socialist Party, which in Europe at that time was not a terribly radical thing to do. But very soon after that, Ho switched views and joined the Communist Party. And that was indeed radical. While the socialists believed in government ownership of industry, communists argued for an almost complete control of the lives of the people.

Communism was an annoying but powerless political concept until 1917, when, in the midst of World War I, a communist government took control of Russia. This event shook the old European order nearly as much as the war did, for Russia had been the home of conservatism. The wealthy and the nobles ruled the nation as though they owned it all. It was the most politically backward nation in Europe, and to find it suddenly changed into a home for radicals was quite a shock.

In 1923, Ho went to Moscow, where he spent at least two years preparing for a return to Vietnam. In 1925, he went to Canton, China, where many Vietnamese nationalists had gone into exile. There he established the Revolutionary Youth League. Ho's group was not large, but its members were well trained and disciplined, and if a vacuum were to come in the leadership of the nationalist movement, Ho and his followers were ready to fill it.

In 1930 the opportunity came. The Vietnam Quoc Dan

Dong (the Vietnam Nationalist Party or "VNQDD") set off a rebellion in the north that was quickly crushed. The VNQDD leaders were executed or imprisoned by the hundreds, and Ho's newly formed Indochinese Communist Party moved in to take over the leadership of the nationalist movement.

The 1930 revolt is an important event, not so much in what happened, for it was just one of many failed revolts in Vietnam, but in the lesson that can be drawn from it. The VNQDD was a fairly moderate organization, yet the French opposed it and eventually destroyed it. They did this because they wanted to hold the colonies they had in Indochina. Yet history and common sense should have told them that they had very little chance of doing this.

The Vietnamese had a very important advantage. They did not have to capture and control Vietnam. They already controlled most of it except for French military outposts. All they had to do was to make it so uncomfortable for the French that staying and fighting would not be worth the trouble. The success of the nationalist movement might be put off for decades but it would come.

In destroying the moderate VNQDD, the French destroyed the last group that they might have made a good deal with; one that would have allowed them a major role in the economy of Vietnam. Destroying the VNQDD could not and would not end the nationalist movement. Rather, it pushed the remaining moderate nationalists into the camp of the Indochinese Communist Party, a far more radical group that would not settle with the French for a small price.

The French must have had some idea of the trouble they were in, because in the next year they brought the boy-emperor Bao Dai back from France, where he had been studying, and they established a Commission of Reforms headed by the Vietnamese Ngo Dinh Diem. While Diem (whose name we shall see again) made a genuine effort to bring reform into the colony, the French blocked all of his efforts and he quickly resigned his position.

The Commission of Reforms was another major French mistake that would be repeated in later years. The idea may have attracted the interest of moderate Vietnamese nationalists for a while, but when it proved to be no more than a trick, any confidence that they had in the French disappeared with it.

This was unfortunate for the French. The series of small storms that were to join to form World War II had already begun to stir. Hitler had come to power in Germany. Mussolini ruled Italy and was invading Ethiopia. And the Japanese had launched their plan to create a huge Asian empire by invading the Chinese province of Manchuria.

In 1939, war broke out in Europe, and while Japan was not involved in that fighting, it was allied to Germany, a nation whose troops would soon be storming across the French border. The French feared for their position in Vietnam for two reasons: First, their main goal was to beat back any German invasion. To do that they had to commit all possible military resources to the defense of France. This left them militarily weak in Indochina.

Second, they feared that any weakness in Asia would

open the door to the Japanese, and in this they were quite correct.

France fell to the invading Germans on June 16, 1940. The surrender terms allowed a French government, under strict German control, to rule most of the nation and its colonies. The government was called "Vichy" France from the town where it had its seat.

After the fall of France, the Japanese sent troops into Vietnam. The Vietnamese nationalist leaders expected that the Japanese would support their aims. But, as once before, when the Japanese had sold out the nationalists for a loan from France, they were disappointed.

If anything, the Vietnamese were in worse trouble than they had been before. The Japanese worked with the governors appointed by the Vichy French government. In effect, they supervised their work. So instead of dealing with one set of colonial masters, the Vietnamese now had to contend with two. Opposition of any sort was brutally put down and what had seemed like the great opportunity for nationalist dreams in Vietnam turned instead into a nightmare.

It seemed as if the Vietnamese were alone against the whole world, and in many ways they were. Even Ho Chi Minh must have given up hope for a moment, for his former friends in Moscow were allied at the beginning of the war with Germany, which of course supported both the Vichy French and the Japanese.

But there were other forces at work. Many French resented the Japanese presence because they regarded Japan as the enemy of France. They worked quietly to liberalize colonial rule and to provide an opportunity for the nationalists to cause trouble for the Japanese and the Vichy French.

Ho Chi Minh, once more in exile in China, formed a new nationalist organization called the Viet Nam Doc Lap Dong Minh—or the Viet Minh. This group would last and would leave its mark in Vietnamese history.

FOUR

The Indochina War

Indochina is more than Vietnam. It is the other nations of Southeast Asia as well. Much was going on in those lands that was similar to what was happening in Vietnam. The Indochina War is a term that properly includes all of the conflicts in that peninsula during this time. But in this chapter, as elsewhere in this book, we will use the term Indochina to mean French-ruled Vietnam and the Indochina War will refer to the struggle that took place between the French and the Vietnamese between the end of World War II and the surrender of French forces in 1954.

Another term used frequently before will have to change in this chapter because it was no longer (as of the 1940s) an appropriate term. That term is "nationalists." The word from now on will be "revolutionaries." The change is for two reasons. First, nationalism was no longer just a political idea, to be talked and written about; it was a revolution, an armed attack against the ruling class.

Second, this revolution was led by Ho Chi Minh and his supporters. Ho was a communist. Whether he was a nationalist first and a communist second or just the opposite is a matter of much debate. Indeed, it is one of the unanswered questions mentioned in the introduction. But he was a communist, and the movement that he led, the goal that he hoped to reach, was not just a free and independent Vietnam, but a Vietnam in which the society and economy would be in line with the principles of Marx and Lenin. His would be a "revolutionary" Vietnam.

How many of his followers wanted something different or did not care if Vietnam was communist or not, so long as it was free, is the subject of another debate that we need not get into. It does not really matter much. The mistakes that were made by Western powers in Vietnam would still be mistakes whether the Viet Minh were more communist or more nationalist. The only difference is that if the Viet Minh were more nationalist than communist, then the Western mistakes were bigger ones.

But let us accept what the major powers all accepted. The United States and France accepted Ho as a communist revolutionary. The Chinese and the Russians did also. If they were all wrong, then Ho was a more complicated man than he appeared, and he appeared to be very complicated indeed. With all this in mind, let us return to Southeast Asia.

World War II was a terrible period for the people of Vietnam. In addition to the difficulties imposed by being caught in the middle of a war and being occupied by two nations, it was also a period of great floods that damaged the rice crop. It is estimated that between one and two million Vietnamese died of starvation between 1940 and 1945.

Life was no less difficult to the north in China. The leader of that nation was Chiang Kaishek and he too had two enemies—the Japanese, who had invaded in 1939, and the Communist Chinese under the leadership of Mao Zedong. All three parties struggled to control that great elephant of a nation and struggled against each other. Chiang hardly knew which enemy to fight first. Shortly after Ho Chi Minh's arrival in China, Chiang had him jailed as a communist.

In 1943, though, Chiang's American advisors persuaded him to release Ho on the theory that he could be of help against the Japanese in Indochina. Their feeling was that Japan was the immediate enemy and that anyone who would cause trouble for Japan was their friend, for the moment at least. To aid this new ally they also convinced Chiang to supply Ho with $100,000 a month. Ho used these funds to build up the Viet Minh as a military force.

The Americans also used Ho as a source of information about Japanese activities. In light of what was to happen a few years later, this may seem strange. But in 1943, Russia was America's ally against Nazi Germany, and the fear of communism, which was to be a central fact in American foreign policy in the late 1940s and early 1950s, had not yet become a major factor.

In addition, there was the attitude of Franklin Delano Roosevelt. President Roosevelt felt that European colonialism was a major cause of World War II. He had determined that at the end of the war he would push for independence for the French colonies, particularly Vietnam. But Roosevelt was nothing if not a practical man. As the United States and its allies gained control in both Europe and the Pacific, he began to meet with other allied leaders about the postwar situation.

In those meetings Vietnam was small potatoes. The Russians were moving toward Germany and were taking control of the Eastern European nations. German defeat was certain, but postwar control of Germany was an open question that divided the allies. The fate of a far-off Asian land was not something that a seriously ill Roosevelt was going to fight with his allies about. He needed their support on other matters, and he was not going to waste that support on less important things.

As 1945 came and the war was coming to a close, the Americans had no real policy about Vietnam. Officially the allies supported continuing French rule in Indochina. Unofficially, the American government was taking steps to make a French return to power difficult, and it was clear that the American agents in Vietnam would be just as happy if Ho Chi Minh ended up leading an independent Vietnam at war's end.

In this they had a strange ally—Japan. A major factor in Japan's going to war was its desire to establish an

Asia ruled by Asians. While they had hoped that those Asians would be Japanese, they also preferred any Asians to continuing European control.

Events came to a head in the spring of 1945. The Japanese had begun to sense defeat, though, since they did not know of the atomic bomb, they must have felt that they had more time than they did. Their German allies were in their last effort and France was free of German control. Japan decided to end the phony French control over Vietnam.

On March 9, the Japanese disarmed and imprisoned the French forces in Vietnam and declared it to be a free nation under the rule of Emperor Bao Dai and under the protection of Japan. The Viet Minh refused to accept the new regime and Ho Chi Minh formed the National Liberation Army.

The United States was not going to send troops to Vietnam to move out the Japanese. America was too busy with its plans to invade Japan for that. But America was very interested in having local forces tie down the Japanese troops in Indochina. The more Japanese troops tied down in Indochina, the fewer would be available in Japan.

In April, Major Archimedes Patti of the Office of Strategic Services (later to become the Central Intelligence Agency) went to northern Vietnam from China and met with Ho Chi Minh. Major Patti was impressed with Ho and began supplying arms to him. Soon a small group of Americans were training Ho's people and going on joint missions with them against the Japanese.

By August of 1945, the National Liberation Army had

established control over the northern parts of Vietnam. When the Japanese surrendered in that month, a group of noncommunist nationalists, the United National Front, took control in the south.

What neither of the Vietnamese groups realized was that the Allies had already met and decided the fate of Vietnam. At the Potsdam Conference in July, it had been agreed by America, Britain and Russia that British troops would take over the Japanese territories in Southeast Asia and that, when order was restored, the French colonies would be returned to the French.

Of course, the British troops did not arrive immediately after the Japanese surrender. So, in late August there were three competing leaders of a "free" Vietnam. Ho Chi Minh in the north, the Emperor Bao Dai in the central region, and the United National Front in the south. Bao Dai knew he could not hold power by himself since he was not liked by the people. He chose Ho as the stronger of his two rivals and declared him to be the head of the Democratic Republic of Vietnam.

For the first time in his life Ho Chi Minh entered the city of Hanoi. He established his capital there and announced that while Vietnam was now a free nation, it would retain strong ties with France. But that was not enough for the French. British troops landed in Saigon on September 12, and French troops followed ten days later. Ho's rule over a free and united Vietnam lasted less than a month.

The French moved quickly to remove Ho's authority in the south, but they left him alone in the north for a while. Just as in the original French takeover, they

brought the south under their control first and dealt
with the problems of the Japanese prisoners still in
Vietnam.

Ho had his own problems in the north though, for
there were two hundred thousand Chinese troops in his
region. Faced with the fact that the French would
eventually turn north and the fact that the Chinese
were already there, Ho made the best deal that he could.
He agreed to have fifteen thousand French troops move
into the north on the condition that the Chinese would
leave. While Ho may have feared the French, he remembered that the Chinese were the oldest and most dangerous enemy of Vietnam.

There began a period of uneasy peace. Though neither
side was completely aware of it, the future of Vietnam
and the lives of millions of people were at stake in the
discussions that took place during this time.

The discussions seemed to go well. The French accepted the idea of a free Vietnam with close political and
business ties to France. They agreed to withdraw their
troops by 1952. The Viet Minh, in turn, agreed to stop
all military activities against the French. This agreement
took place in March of 1946. By June it had been
broken, for in that month Frenchmen living in Vietnam
had decided that they wanted no part of the deal. They
must have realized that an independent Vietnam would
mean an end to their large estates and their complete
control over business. They wanted a French-owned
South Vietnam.

This group of French businessmen declared an independent Republic of Cochinchina. The discussions

started again. This time, though, the results were different. The north of Vietnam would be allowed some independence but not complete freedom, and there would be no unified Vietnam.

This agreement was doomed from the start. Signed in September, it was gone before Christmas. How and why the shooting started is not clear. But minor battles soon turned into serious conflicts. The leak in the truce became a flood on December 19, 1946, when the French bombarded the city of Haiphong, killing six thousand Vietnamese.

Ho knew that his new and poorly equipped army could not defeat French troops who had been fighting in Europe for years. So he decided to avoid a major battle until he had the power to win one. He pulled back his troops from Hanoi into the country and waited—for eight years.

The military parts of the Viet Minh were under the control of a former history professor named Vo Nguyen Giap. He and Ho planned a strategy that would annoy the French, keep the idea of rebellion in the minds of the Vietnamese people and would depend on the great strength of the Viet Minh: their knowledge of Vietnam and its people. Over the next three years they put their idea to work. The Viet Minh were armed, trained and sent off into the country.

They existed everywhere in the north, but were nowhere to be seen. There were no uniforms, medals or badges. They were just there, attacking the French when and where they least expected it and moving swiftly back into their villages. There was no way to fight them because there was no way to find them. So long as they were better liked in their villages than were the French, they were safe, for no one would tell the French who they were.

For more than four years this "guerrilla" warfare was kept up. The French were not only annoyed, they were spending a lot of money on what was, after all, supposed to be a money-making colony. They longed for the opportunity to fight the Viet Minh out in the open—the type of battle they knew about and believed that they could win. But General Giap held his forces back. He was not going to fight the French on their terms until the moment that he was sure that he could win. That moment would come soon.

Two things took place in early 1950 that made Giap more sure of himself. First, the Chinese Communists had won their own revolution the year before and had recognized Ho Chi Minh's government as the true government of Vietnam. That meant that just to the north was a powerful and now friendly neighbor who could supply military as well as political aid.

Second, the Korean War had broken out. Korea, a former Japanese colony, had been broken into two parts at the end of World War II. In the spring of 1950, the communist-controlled north invaded the south. The United Nations sided with the south, and large numbers of American and other United Nations troops were involved in the fighting. The Chinese supported the North Koreans with troops as well as arms. The war ended in pretty much a tie. The original borders were kept. In large part the tie was due to American unwillingness to attack China. To Ho and General Giap, the events in Korea must have been very interesting. One conclusion that they could have drawn was that the people of Europe and the United States were not happy about a war that seemed to drag on forever with no clear winner in a land that was far from home and had not even appeared in their school history books.

But another idea that they could have had and probably did not was that the Korean War deeply upset the American people. The communist takeover in China had set off a tide of strong anticommunism in the United States. The lack of victory in Korea was upsetting for a country that had just beaten Germany, Japan and Italy in World War II.

Because of these two facts, elected officials in the United States could not ever seem to give in to communists. But the Viet Minh must not have seen this or, if they did, they went ahead despite it. In 1950, Giap went on the offensive. His first efforts at open battles were not always successful. The French were growing stronger since the United States had started to pour large amounts of money into the French military effort. Starting with $10 million in 1950, American military aid rose to $1 billion by 1954.

Giap started slowly, attacking a small French camp near the Chinese border—Dong Khe. Two hundred French Legionnaires were defeated there in September of 1950. The next month he attacked French forces near Cao Bang. Of the ten thousand French troops, six thousand were killed, wounded or captured.

But by the new year, Giap was not doing so well.

Throughout 1951, Giap was defeated several times by French troops. No victory was lasting, though, since the French had to keep to the roads. Their modern military equipment gave them a great advantage in an open battle, but once they had defeated the Viet Minh, their opponents went off into the forests and mountains where French tanks and artillery could not follow them.

At this point the French should have begun to realize that they were caught in what had been properly described as a "quicksand war"—one in which they stepped on what seemed to be solid ground, only to find that they were sinking quickly into the mud.

The French finally reached this conclusion and tried to convince the United States of it. But as we shall see, the United States did not agree with the French view.

Indeed, by 1953, when the French had suffered seventy-four thousand casualties and had two hundred and fifty thousand troops in Vietnam, the French military had decided that the war was hopeless. But France was a proud nation and its military leaders remembered very clearly the swift defeat of the French army by the Germans early in World War II. They wanted to show that France was stronger than it had seemed in that war.

They believed that if they could only force the Viet Minh out into the open, they could win a military victory that would allow France to begin the process of seeking an honorable peace. They were willing to quit but they wanted to quit when they were ahead.

There were those who thought that nothing would make the French effort in Indochina honorable. One of them was a young American senator who visited Vietnam in late 1951. On his return he said, "In Indochina we have allied ourselves to the desperate effort of the French regime to hang on to the remnants of an empire."

The speaker was John F. Kennedy.

But the French were set in their ways, and by late 1953, that course had led them on the road to a small and not very important Vietnamese village called Dien Bien Phu.

A young Cho Minh speaks about the reunion of Vietnam. Ho spent fifty years of his life trying to achieve this goal, but died shortly before reaching it.

President Eisenhower and Secretary of State Dulles greet President Diem of South Vietnam. It was in the 1950s, during Eisenhower's administration, that the United States first became heavily involved in Vietnam.

Above: Toward the end of his life President Kennedy seemed to have begun to doubt the wisdom of American involvement in Vietnam. Here he meets with General Maxwell Taylor and Secretary of Defense Robert McNamara in the Oval Office.

Below: Lyndon Johnson took over from the assassinated Kennedy. Under his leadership the American involvement grew rapidly. Here he is shown greeting Prime Minister Ky of South Vietnam while President Thieu shakes hands with McNamara and Secretary of State Rusk, two Kennedy aides who stayed on to work for L.B.J.

Presidents and cabinet members were not the only noncombatant Americans to go to Vietnam. In the upper photo, comedian Bob Hope tries out the controls of an American cargo plane while on a wartime visit. In the lower photo, a Red Cross volunteer joins in a Christmas celebration.

An older and more weary Ho Chi Minh is shown near the
time of his death in 1969.

FIVE

A Tale of Two Cities

Dien Bien Phu and Geneva

There are probably no two places less alike than the cities of Geneva, Switzerland, and Dien Bien Phu. But in 1954, the two places came together in a way that was to cause the destruction of one and a decision on the fate of Indochina in the other. Let us look first at Dien Bien Phu.

It was and is a crossroads town. It is located where three main highways join in northwestern Vietnam just ten miles from the Laotian border. The Viet Minh received much of their supplies from China through supply routes from Laos.

In 1953, a new commander of French troops arrived in Vietnam. His name was General Henri Navarre, and like those who came before him, he wished strongly to force the Viet Minh into a major open battle. He felt that a major French force at Dien Bien Phu would draw out the Viet Minh, who would have to battle there in order to secure their Laotian supply lines.

The Korean War had ended in July of 1953, and that fact put pressure on Navarre. The end of the war had caused two changes in the situation in Vietnam. First, the Chinese were no longer caught up in Korea and so were able to send greater amounts of military supplies to the Viet Minh, making them a more formidable enemy. The longer Navarre waited, the stronger his opponents would be. Second, the truce in Korea created an atmosphere in which the search for a political settlement in Vietnam was more important than ever. Westerners were tired of war in Asia. In 1953, the Viet Minh controlled enough of Vietnam to be able to ask a lot in any political settlement. Navarre's task was to improve the military situation so that France's position in any political bargaining would be increased.

Late in a football game, when your team is behind by four points, the other team will allow you to get a field goal because they want to stop you from getting a touchdown. Your team would be happy with either a touchdown or two field goals. Navarre was behind by ten points and he wanted a touchdown so the game would be close.

In late November, Navarre began to send paratroops into Dien Bien Phu. His information was that there were no Viet Minh in the area. His information was wrong.

Of the first eight hundred French troops to land in the town, forty were killed by two companies of Viet Minh. However, the French soon secured the area and by the end of the month had ten thousand troops in place.

Their first task was to build airstrips, for all of their supplies would have to be brought in by plane. The town was a hundred and seventy rugged miles from Hanoi and was in a hollow surrounded by heavily wooded hills. The French knew that the terrain would prevent them from bringing in any heavy equipment on the ground and believed that it would have the same effect on the Viet Minh.

The French were wrong again.

General Giap, too, saw Dien Bien Phu as a great opportunity, and he developed a plan with four parts to it to take advantage of the situation.

First he gathered a peasant army of some twenty thousand people whose main job would be to cut supply roads through the forests for troops and supplies to move on. These were little more than simple trails, but that was all that was needed. Second, on these trails the trained army troops would move in as quickly as possible, traveling day and night. If the French had known of these two parts of the plan, they would not have been greatly concerned. After all, the reason they came to Dien Bien Phu was to fight the Viet Minh after having drawn large numbers of them to one place.

They expected to win such a battle because the Viet Minh would not have artillery and because they would not be able to supply large numbers of troops for any long period of time.

The Viet Minh had very few trucks, and the French could easily close off the roads to any vehicles while they brought their own supplies by air. But the Viet Minh did not use trucks or roads or airplanes. They used bicycles. This was the third part of the plan.

Throughout northern Vietnam orders were received to prepare what the Vietnamese called *xe tho*. The frame of an ordinary bicycle was strengthened so that it could hold up to four hundred pounds of supplies. A bamboo pole was attached to the handlebars to allow the bike to be steered by someone walking along side it and another pole was attached to the seat to provide a balance point. The tires were strengthened by wrapping them with cloth strips cut from the trouser legs of the peasants.

Thousands of *xe tho* set off for Dien Bien Phu along the new paths pushed by thousands of Vietnamese who were now wearing shorts. By the beginning of 1954, the French had reason to be concerned. They knew the Viet Minh were in the hills and that they (the French), were tied down in the valley until the fighting began. But they were not overly concerned because they did not know how many troops were opposing them; they did not think that these troops had enough supplies; and they were confident that the Viet Minh had no heavy weapons while they themselves had twenty-eight large artillery pieces.

In fact, though, the Viet Minh had almost two hundred artillery units. Each one had been pulled by armies of peasants through the narrow paths and up the hills surounding Dien Bien Phu. An inch at a time, a half-mile a day, they crept toward Dien Bien Phu. It took three months to move them fifty miles. By late February they were all in place. This was the fourth part of the plan.

And General Giap waited. He would not move until victory was sure. But by mid-March events were closing in on Giap and forcing his hand.

A conference was scheduled to begin in Geneva in late spring to work out a cease-fire agreement in Indochina. Just as the French saw Dien Bien Phu as an opportunity to enter political discussions with a strong military position, so did Giap see the coming conference as a deadline. If he were to win an important battle against the French in the open field, then Viet Minh negotiators could claim that the French position was hopeless and demand a better political settlement.

The Viet Minh had come silently and invisibly to Dien Bien Phu. On March 12, 1954, they were seen and heard all too clearly. Shortly after five in the afternoon two hundred artillery pieces let loose from the five hills around the French camp. For more than an hour they blasted away at the airstrip and the French camp. When the guns had stopped, the infantry followed the path the shells had taken. One of the seven French strongpoints fell quickly with five hundred of its seven hundred defenders killed. In the next two days two more strongpoints surrendered to Viet Minh assaults.

On March 16, French paratroopers reinforced the troops at Dien Bien Phu. The fresh troops helped a little. The Vietnamese were pushed back slightly, but the French suffered heavy losses in the effort, and this they could not afford. There would be no more reinforcements. The Viet Minh artillery had destroyed the airport and the shrinking French position was not large enough for paratroopers to land in safety.

Even worse, the closing of the airstrip meant that the French wounded could not be taken out. At Dien Bien Phu there were twelve thousand French troops. The medical team was composed of four doctors and one nurse, Genevieve de Galard. In order to survive, the French had to retake some of their lost territory. Supplies were desperately needed, but much of what was dropped by parachute was landing in Viet Minh hands.

In early April, the French fired all of their mortars and artillery at one Viet Minh position. Then they attacked and fought the Viet Minh hand-to-hand. Slowly they gained ground, but not enough. More than two thousand men were killed on each side and very little had been gained. Nonetheless General Giap was greatly worried. He had lost almost ten thousand troops, who had been killed or wounded. He did not want to lose many more. His troops were unhappy at their heavy losses. The Viet Minh medical situation was even worse than the French. Rather than lose the support of his troops, Giap decided to change his tactics. His soldiers put down their rifles and picked up their shovels. They began to dig trenches toward Dien Bien Phu.

Slowly the miles of tunnel inched toward the French positions. Only an attack from the air could stop or slow the progress, but the French did not have the equipment for this. The United States did, and President Eisenhower considered sending bombers to support the French. Indeed, Richard Nixon, who was then vice-president, wrote that the United States military had drawn a plan that would include the use of small atomic weapons. Perhaps because of Congressional opposition, including that of Senators Lyndon Johnson and John Kennedy, the American aid plan was never carried out.

The Viet Minh came out of the ground on May 6 and made good progress. When they attacked again on May 7, the French simply stopped fighting. Dien Bien Phu was lost and only further deaths would be gained from continuing.

The eight weeks of battle at Dien Bien Phu had caught the attention of the world. French troops in a far-off corner of the world were holding on against impossible odds, opposed by an enemy that was obviously brave and very skilled at the art of war. This was the stuff of newspaper headlines. When joined with the endless efforts of Genevieve de Galard to save lives and ease pain, one can easily understand that no other event in the world was so closely watched at the time as the battle of Dien Bien Phu.

But thousands of miles away on the hilly shores of Lake Geneva in Switzerland another story was unfolding that was not nearly as exciting as that of Dien Bien Phu, but was in many ways more important.

Geneva is a strange city. Certainly it is as different from Dien Bien Phu as could be. Until 1815, it was an independent republic. In that year it joined the Confederation of Switzerland, which is itself an unusual nation. Surrounded by land and surrounded by Germany, Austria, Italy and France, the Swiss use three different languages (French, Italian, and German). Despite its position in the middle of some of the most powerful nations in Europe, Switzerland has chosen to remain neutral in all wars since 1815 and other nations have

respected that, even in the middle of World War I and
World War II.

Because of this neutral position, Switzerland has often
been chosen as the headquarters for international organizations such as the Red Cross. It has also often been
the meeting place for important international con-
ferences.

Just such a conference met in that city on April 27,
1954. Its purpose was to discuss a cease-fire in Indochina. But this meant more than discussing the military
aspects of that war. All parties knew that an agreement
on a military cease-fire would have to include some
political decisions. In other words, the parties had not
met to say, "Everyone will stop fighting on July 17 at
noon." They also had to discuss which Vietnamese group
would rule in what part of the country. The Viet Minh
controlled important parts of South Vietnam by military
force. These parts were under the political control of the
French-sponsored government in Saigon. Some decision
had to be made as to who was really in charge.

At the conference were Great Britain, France, the
United States, the Soviet Union, Communist China, Cambodia, Laos, South Vietnam and the Viet Minh. When
we use the name "South Vietnam" at this point in this
story, we mean the French-sponsored puppet government which, on paper at least, ruled the entire nation. In
fact it ruled only in parts of the south and in some small
parts of the north around Hanoi.

The French, British, Russians and Chinese came to
Geneva with fairly similar ideas in mind. All expected
that the conference would agree on a plan whereby
Vietnam would be temporarily divided between north

and south. The fighting would stop and troops would return home. The nation, at some future time, would be made one again by elections.

Unfortunately, two countries were against the plan: the United States and South Vietnam. Their reasons were the same. Both believed that national elections would result in a Viet Minh victory. In fact, everyone expected that that would happen. The French certainly did, and they were ready to deal with a Ho Chi Minh government after the war.

The American felt that such a victory would be because the Viet Minh would convince people that the South Vietnamese government was really just another French government. The Viet Minh would picture themselves as the true nationalists and the election would be seen by the people of Vietnam as a contest between the French (South Vietnam) and the nationalists (Viet Minh). To the Americans, this was seen as a trick, but in fact it was very close to the truth. While the leaders of South Vietnam were not just tools of the French, they were Catholic, like the French; they spoke French and wore Western clothing. If they did not want to be ruled by the French, they certainly wanted to be like them. Whatever else the Viet Minh were—communists, Russians or Chinese agents—they were also the only strong nationalist group in the nation, the only ones with broad popular support.

Part of the United States government also felt that a military victory over the Viet Minh was still possible. Unfortunately, that part was the State Department. The military leaders in the United States did not share that view. And the State Department had special reasons for wanting to believe in a military victory. That department was blamed by many for the communist takeover in China and for allowing the Korean War to end up about where it had started after a great loss of life. The department and its leader, Secretary of State John Foster Dulles, were deeply worried about being labeled as "soft on Communism."

The State Department was not just worried about what people thought about it, though. Communist forces had taken over much of Eastern Europe after 1946, and the Korean War itself began when the communist North Koreans invaded South Korea. Fears about communist imperialism were based on very recent events. The French felt, though, that Vietnam was a special case. Their view was that Ho Chi Minh was a nationalist first and that by careful negotiation at Geneva they could keep the century-old French relationship with Vietnam even under communist leadership. Moreover, they were not as sure as the United States that a communist government in Vietnam would try to expand its power over all of Indochina and into other parts of Southeast Asia.

This concern about expansion of communist influence was known as the "domino" theory. The idea was that if Vietnam fell, the other nations in the areas would tip over like dominoes. It was to avoid this result that the United States had spent four billion dollars in support of the French military effort.

The United States came to Geneva with the idea in mind that it would convince its major allies, France and

Great Britain, to oppose a division of Vietnam. It proposed instead that the three nations join in opposition to any possibility of communist control. Such a union would include possible joint military action.

It soon became clear, though, that the American plan was not acceptable to its allies. That meant that any agreement coming out of Geneva would involve a temporary division followed by elections, which was what the other countries wanted. Since such a plan meant a communist takeover, the United States took steps to remove itself as a visible party in Geneva. The American group sent its highest ranking member away from Geneva. In this way Dulles felt that he could avoid the impression that America was bound by any agreement reached. The United States would not take part in the Geneva Conference. It would just be an observer.

At least that was what the public saw. While it is true that the United States did not talk directly with its "opponents"—the communist countries—it is also true that the United States made its position known to France and Great Britain. These American views had a great effect on the positions taken by its friends. The United States was having it both ways. It looked as if it had walked out of the conference and was free to say that it did not approve any agreement reached in Geneva. At the same time it was saying to its allies "we do not like this idea of dividing the country and holding elections, but if that is what you are going to do, here is how we would like to have you do it."

This type of negotiation is common and not as evil as it may sound. If there was someone you were not talking to, but you needed them to do something for a team or club, you might have another person talk to them for you. That would not be very different from what the United States was doing. The United States had a goal that it knew it could not reach at Geneva. The failure to reach that goal meant that the United States wanted to be free to take other actions to reach it. In order to have that freedom, it could not be seen as agreeing to the results in Geneva. But it also had an interest in seeing to it that Geneva ended as favorably as possible from the American point of view.

In private then, the United States told its allies that it would "respect" a division of Vietnam. That is, it would not publicly support a division, but it would not fight against it. In fact, the main American concern as the negotiations neared an end in July was the possibility of elections. The United States's position was that elections should be delayed as long as possible. No date should be set for a vote. The American view was that Ho Chi Minh would easily win any election held in the near future. It was hoped that, by delaying the election, democratic forces in South Vietnam would gain enough support among the people to win later on. What Secretary of State Dulles did not realize was that what America was hoping for was a lot like looking for somebody to run against George Washington at the end of the American Revolution. Anyone foolish enough to run was certainly not able to win.

The final agreement did not make the State Department happy. The four main parts of the agreement were: a division of Vietnam along the seventeenth parallel (roughly in the middle of the nation); elections to be held in July of 1956 for the purpose of reuniting the nation; a three-nation International Control Commission consisting of India, Canada and Poland to control the cease-fire and the elections; and the removal of all French troops within three hundred days. No new troops from foreign nations were to be brought in.

The United States and South Vietnam did not sign the agreement. Instead each nation made a statement. The American statement said two rather strange things. First, that it would "refrain from the threat or use of force to disturb" the agreements. Second, that it would look at any violations with grave concern. The statements are odd because the first seems to say that the United States would fully respect the agreement, which is quite close to approving it. The second part hints that the United States would use force to make sure the agreement was followed. The Americans were saying that they accepted, as they had to, the heart of the agreement but that they were keeping their options open.

Maybe, the best way to sum up the American position is by saying that the United States was not happy about the agreement, but would not use force to oppose it unless someone else broke the agreement, in which case the United States was ready to act.

The South Vietnam reaction was more direct. That government simply rejected the agreement and refused to be bound by it. In later years there would be a lot of argument about whether the South Vietnamese had not actually agreed to be bound by some parts of the document. While a chapter could be spent on that debate, it is fair to say that South Vietnam was never legally or morally bound by the agreement. By French treaty, Vietnam had been a free nation since June 4. While that freedom was allowed for political reasons, it made South Vietnam a nation. No other nation's actions could bind it, and it did not bind itself.

Dien Bien Phu and Geneva ended one phase of the story of Vietnam and began another. In that phase the United States would become a major party in a war that was more visible than any in history. It was seen and heard every night on television throughout the world. Hundreds of thousands of Americans fought in it and as many fought against it.

It is odd then that the next phase begins with one man acting behind the scenes and earning himself the nickname "the Quiet American."

SIX

A Tale of Two Presidents

Diem and Kennedy

A month before the Geneva agreements were signed, Colonel Edward C. Lansdale arrived in Saigon, where he had been sent by the American Secretary of State, John Foster Dulles. He was to head the Central Intelligence Agency office in Vietnam. Lansdale was a remarkable man. His life and his work were wrapped up in the idea of democracy. But he was not just a street-corner preacher. He was a very practical man who had shown that he could do what he said he would do. His soft-spoken approach had earned him the nickname "the

Quiet American." His mission was to save Vietnam from communism.

At the end of World War II, he had been sent to the Philippines to do the same thing. That nation, which had recently ended a half-century as an American colony, was facing a serious rebellion led by communists. Lansdale worked closely with Filipino leaders to fight the rebellion through both political and military means. He had succeeded because he was able to convince the government that its best tool against the rebels was to listen to what they said needed to be done—and then to do it. In the Philippines he had picked one leader, Ramon Magsaysay, and became his friend and aide. In Vietnam he planned to do the same thing and he chose Ngo Dinh Diem. That was a great mistake and, in a way, very surprising.

Just ten years before, you remember, the CIA (then known as the OSS) had sent Major Patti to Vietnam. That officer had decided that Ho Chi Minh was the man to back in Vietnam and the United States had done so. The French at that time had been greatly opposed to Ho, of course. Now, after nearly ten years of war, the French had accepted the idea that Ho had the support of the Vietnamese people and that they could deal with him. The United States had also made a complete turnaround. Ho was no longer a nationalist patriot but a communist revolutionary. The United States would oppose him with all its might and would put its hope in Diem.

Lansdale saw Diem as someone very much like his Filipino friend, Magsaysay. Diem was a genuine patriot who was personally honest and who had a dream for his nation's future. These were certainly good qualities to look for if one was searching, as Lansdale was, for a national leader who would provide a choice between French colonial rule and a communist takeover.

But Diem and Magsaysay were not completely alike. Diem was a Catholic in a country where Catholics were a small group in the great Buddhist population. Magsaysay was a Catholic, also, but so were most of his countrymen. Diem came from the Vietnamese nobility. He was a mandarin, while Magsaysay's roots were in the rural parts of the Philippines. Diem kept to himself. He was almost a hermit, while Magsaysay had a strong and popular personality.

The man closest to the Magsaysay model in Vietnam was Ho Chi Minh and between him and Diem there was another big difference. Through his many years of fighting and power Ho had gained nothing for himself. He dressed as a peasant and lived simply. Diem too lived simply, but his many friends and relatives used their power to gain great wealth. While Diem himself was not corrupt, he allowed those close to him to become wealthy at the expense of the people.

All of this is easy to see thirty years later. But Lansdale arrived in Vietnam on an urgent mission and he did not have the time to look around for future national leaders. The man who was there, Diem, seemed all right to Lansdale even though he had some problems that had to be overcome. Lansdale made his choice and his choice was Diem. Through him and with him Lansdale set about on his mission—stopping a Communist victory in Vietnam.

Diem had been made Prime Minister of South Vietnam on July 7, 1954, by Emperor Bao Dai. The French had given political freedom to the nation just before the Geneva agreements were signed. The agreements were to be followed by a temporary division of the nation during the first three months of which there would be a "free travel" period in which persons could move freely between north and south—selecting which half of the country they would live in. They would be "voting" with their feet.

Both sides tried hard to attract people to their half of the nation. Diem made his pitch to the Catholic population in the north with the slogan "God has gone south." This scheme was joined with a CIA plan designed to frighten French businessmen in the north. Both schemes worked and large numbers of Catholics moved south (as did many Viet Minh agents) and most French businesses pulled out of Vietnam. All told, eight hundred and fifty thousand Vietnamese moved south and only eighty thousand went north.

The plan was a disaster as far as the French were concerned. Their hopes for friendly relations with Ho Chi Minh were ruined by the loss of a friendly Catholic population and French business interests in the north. The French felt strongly that the United States was pushing Ho Chi Minh further into the communist camp by taking away his Western allies.

The United States was aware of the problems in their plan. The American ambassador in Vietnam warned the State Department in late 1954 that he had serious doubts about the people's support for Diem. Secretary Dulles answered that "there is no other suitable leader known to us." The United States would make do with what it had—Diem.

Lansdale's hope was that he could quickly make Diem a national hero and give him an opportunity to win the elections set by the Geneva agreement for July of 1956. Of course, since both the United States and South Vietnam had refused to sign those agreements, they were not bound by the elections. But if those elections could be won by Diem, it was good for both nations to let them go on. This might avoid a civil war and show that democracy could win out over communism in a free election. Lansdale used many tricks to build up Diem and cut down Ho. Among these was the publication in Hanoi of a fortune-telling book. The Vietnamese are a superstitious people, and this particular book said that if Ho were to win the election, disaster would befall the Vietnamese people.

But the United States was not so sure of a Diem victory that it gave up the idea of military action. It developed a plan to train and equip a South Vietnamese army and, in February of 1955, established the South East Asia Treaty Organization (SEATO). This group was based on the NATO alliance, which had bound the nations of Western Europe and North America into a common defense alliance after World War II.

SEATO was very different from NATO though. Most of its members were European nations who joined only because America asked them to. While NATO nations really cared about their treaty, SEATO members had nothing at stake. But SEATO did require that member nations defend any other member attacked by any other country. The SEATO treaty would give America a legal right to fight in Vietnam.

With all the players now on stage, the tragedy of Vietnam began again. Diem had no real power. He had been appointed by the very unpopular Emperor Bao Dai. He had not been elected by the people. He tried to make himself stronger by appointing his friends and relatives to the most important government jobs and by beating the criminal gangs who ran much of South Vietnam (including the Saigon Police Department).

To Diem, giving important jobs to his family and friends was not unusual. He believed in a philosophy called "personalism," in which personal relationships are the major force in life. The better you knew someone, the more you should respect them. It was natural, then, for him to surround himself with people chosen for their jobs because of their closeness to him rather than on any special talents they might have had.

At Lansdale's suggestion Diem also called for elections in South Vietnam. These took place in October of 1955 and were intended to strengthen his rule. Diem won the election with a highly suspicious ninety-eight percent of the vote, and then announced that he would not agree to the scheduled national elections because of the chance that they might be rigged by Ho Chi Minh.

While any election held in a country with no history of democracy may be fixed, and while it seems likely that Ho Chi Minh would have been happy to stuff some ballot boxes, Diem's statement was very odd. There can be no question that Ho Chi Minh would have won any honest election. In fact, Ho's victory was seen as certain by President Eisenhower. Diem had not caught on with the people as Lansdale had hoped.

It looked very much as if Diem did not want elections because he did not want to lose. To keep himself in power, he used the secret police headed by his brother, Ngo Dinh Nhu. This brutal organization killed thousands of opponents of Diem's regime. At the same time, in the north, the Viet Minh were killing thousands of their own opponents. If you hope to find good guys in this story, you will be disappointed. There are none.

Diem also tried a softer approach. He presented ideas for land reform that would give the peasants a chance to own their own farms and bring some independence to their lives. Unfortunately, the program was run by Diem's family and friends, who saw it, and took it, as another chance to make some money. At the same time the cost of supporting Diem's friends and family and of raising an army to protect against invasion from the north also caused a great increase in taxes. The higher taxes upset the peasants very much. In villages throughout South Vietnam opposition to Diem increased.

To stop this opposition Diem took a serious step. For centuries, indeed for thousands of years, the village had been the basic unit of Vietnamese life and government. The village was one's world and one's life. Indeed the old Vietnamese word for village, "xa," comes from the words for "land," "people" and "sacred." As we have seen, governments in Vietnam were pretty much powerless except for some phases of French Colonial rule. Diem sought to stop opposition and expand his power by canceling all village elections and naming village chiefs himself. Village independence had been respected by the invading Chinese, French and Japanese. That a native Vietnamese should end it shows that Diem had become desperate or foolish. The opposition to him was silenced for the moment, but it was not ended.

There were no elections in 1956. Ho Chi Minh made some protest about this, but he seems to have known what the International Control Commission set up by the Geneva agreements publicly stated: the Geneva agreements were a failure. Neither side had honored either the military cease-fire or the political parts of it.

The option was clear—war, long and destructive war. In 1957, Diem began to appeal for more American military aid. In part, Diem wanted help to combat his opponents in South Vietnam. But in part, too, his plea was a response to the increased activity of those people whom Diem called the Viet Cong. That name was intended as an insult. It referred to the Viet Minh supporters who lived in the South. But the name stuck and is useful in a way. It will become more important to know that there was a difference between South Vietnamese who opposed the Diem regime (whether they supported Ho Chi Minh or not) and those people who would soon be moving south as invaders. Neither the United States nor any other foreign nation had much business interfering with a native revolt. Certainly SEATO did not. It promised protection only against outside aggression. When outside aggression did take place, then America's right to step in was much clearer, in a legal sense at least. While there is much reason to believe that the Viet Cong in South Vietnam took their orders from Hanoi in the north, that is not completely certain, and so it is helpful to speak of the Viet Cong to describe that group of South Vietnamese who were followers of Ho Chi Minh as well as those who simply opposed the Diem regime in South Vietnam. Later, when the lines are less clear between southern rebels and northern invaders, we will use the initials NLF (National Liberation Front) to describe the southern guerrillas. That was their organization and gives us a way to see these native opponents as different from the North Vietnamese Army.

By 1960, Lansdale had left Vietnam and had been replaced by William Colby as CIA chief. Colby, who later went on to head the CIA during the Nixon administration and to become American ambassador to Iran, launched a new effort called the strategic hamlet program. This program took the Diem mistake about village elections and made it even worse. The village residents were moved out of their homes into fortified camps called strategic hamlets. The hamlets were seen as a means of self-defense against the Viet Cong, who at that time were very busy killing off the village leaders appointed by Diem.

The mistake in the program was that the villagers did not want protection and certainly did not want to be moved from their ancient homes and farms. They did not always necessarily see the Viet Cong as enemies, but as neighbors, friends and family. When night came and the Viet Cong were ready to return home, the villagers opened the gates of their hamlets and let them back in. The program quickly became a joke.

This was so in part because the program was run by the military. That is not to say that the military did not run it well. The problem was that the military naturally act from a military point of view. Their training is in the military way of solving problems. The strategic hamlets were not a military solution; they were to be a way for the villagers to protect themselves without aid from the military. The military leaders, from the first, had very little belief in the program and when they realized that it would be easier to keep the villagers inside the hamlets than to try to keep the Viet Cong out of them, they turned the hamlets into prisons for the people who lived there. Since you could not tell the Viet Cong from other villagers, the simplest way to keep the Viet Cong from wandering around causing trouble was to lock everybody up in the hamlets. This tactic did little to slow the growth in opposition to the Diem regime.

By 1961, America had to make a major decision about Vietnam. Six years had gone by and billions of dollars had been spent and almost nothing had been gained. The American aid was not doing any good, so the Americans had to consider whether to increase that aid or pull out entirely.

The decision fell to John F. Kennedy, who had been inaugurated as president on January 20, 1961. Two things happened on that day that set the course for what was to follow.

First, Kennedy gave a strong inaugural address in which he said:

Let every nation know . . . that we shall pay any price, bear any burden, meet any hardship, support any friend, oppose any foe to assure the survival and success of liberty.

The language is strong and clear. It announced that President Kennedy was going to be active in foreign affairs, something he would show often in his brief term as president.

The second event was much less public. President Eisenhower spoke to Kennedy about Southeast Asia. He told Kennedy that he thought that he would have to send troops to that area and that, if he did, he could count on Eisenhower's public support. Eisenhower was very worried about the situation in Laos, which was similar to what was going on in Vietnam, but with more communist military forces involved. The Laos situation was cleared up rather quickly, though, through an agreement as to who would run the country. If Kennedy were to listen to Eisenhower's warning about Southeast Asia, he would do it in Vietnam.

Eisenhower was not the only leader to give President Kennedy advice about Vietnam. Shortly after his inauguration, Kennedy went to France and met with French President Charles De Gaulle. The French experience in Vietnam was still a painful memory, which was made stronger by the fact that France was now going through the same thing again in its colony in Algeria. DeGaulle told Kennedy, "I predict to you that you will, step by step, be sucked into a bottomless military and political quagmire." DeGaulle was right.

Kennedy took Eisenhower's advice very seriously. The communists' use of force around the world was of real concern to him, but he had problems in trying to stop it. Kennedy had favored a neutral government in Laos, which many people saw as giving an advantage to the communists. He had backed an invasion of Cuba at the Bay of Pigs. When that failed he was criticized for not allowing strong air support for the invaders.

After much thought, he decided to increase American military efforts in Vietnam. In December of 1961, he sent in three hundred helicopter pilots. Within a few months the American military support group had increased to four thousand people.

By 1963, the United States was a real military force in Vietnam, and Kennedy had only eleven months left to live. What would have happened had he lived is one of the unanswered questions about Vietnam. But we can see in what happened in those few months some signs of what he planned to do. The fact that the signs are hard to read shows that Kennedy himself was not sure what he intended, and that probably is the real truth.

Things were taking place in Vietnam that would have made any American leader worry. The Buddhists were becoming more active in their opposition to Diem. This opposition had very little to do with any support for Ho Chi Minh. Nearly ninety-five percent of all Vietnamese were Buddhists and yet Diem would not allow them to practice their religion in peace. Some of his actions were very foolish.

On Buddha's birthday one Buddhist temple flew a religious flag. The secret police removed it. When Buddhists took to the streets to protest, forty of them were killed.

The street protests continued though, and on June 11, 1963, a Buddhist monk named Thich Quang Duc sat down on a Saigon street, poured gasoline all over himself, and set himself on fire as a protest against the Diem regime. The newspapers had been told what would happen, and the awful pictures of the monk sitting on fire in the street were seen throughout the world. President Diem's sister-in-law, Madame Nhu, described the event as a "barbecue." Diem and his family did not understand that the people's problems were real and had to be solved.

While Diem's family may have literally laughed about the burning, President Kennedy was deeply shocked. He began to talk about withdrawing American forces. As a caring person he could not back the things Diem was doing, and as a politician he could not afford another loss in foreign affairs. He began to take steps to show how upset he was.

The American Ambassador to South Vietnam was Frederick Nolting—a Diem supporter. In August, Kennedy replaced him with Henry Cabot Lodge. Lodge was an odd choice in a sense. He was a Republican from Massachusetts (which is a little odd itself) and he had been a United States Senator until he had been defeated by John Kennedy himself. In 1960, he was the Republican candidate for vice-president running with Richard Nixon against the Democratic team of Kennedy and Lyndon Johnson.

But Lodge was a man of great experience in foreign affairs. (He had been Ambassador to the United Nations from 1953 to 1960.) He was also a man of great talent. He would provide the fresh look that Kennedy needed, and Kennedy hoped that his advice would be good.

His first action was to meet with Nolting in Hawaii on his way to Saigon. Nolting told him that the Buddhist problem was over. But while they talked, Buddhist temples all over South Vietnam were being raided, and one thousand four hundred Buddhists were sent to prison. Though no one said it out loud, any person watching what was going on would have known that the United States could no longer aid the Diem government.

Among the people who were watching things closely were the military leaders of South Vietnam. In late August, soon after Lodge arrived in Saigon, word came to him that some of the generals were thinking of overthrowing Diem's government. Lodge asked Washington what he should do. A telegram came back telling him to do two things. First he was to tell Diem that his brother Nhu had to be removed from power as head of the police. Second he was to tell the generals about this and that, if Nhu was not removed, then all American support would be cut off.

The South Vietnamese military needed American military aid. An end to that aid meant a possible invasion from the north. The generals took the telegram as a "green light"—a signal to go ahead with their plans. It may not have been that. The United States was saying that Nhu had to go; it was not yet saying that Diem had to go. But the generals did not believe that Diem would remove his brother from power, and so to them it meant that Diem had to go in order to keep American aid.

Lodge saw the telegram the same way that the generals did, and he told the State Department that an effort to remove Nhu would be useless. Diem would be removed, he told them, and they may as well support it now. The State Department gave Lodge the power to make his own decisions while hoping that the generals and Diem could work out a way to solve the problem of Nhu.

The same day President Kennedy cabled Lodge himself and told Lodge that he would do what he could to help the generals succeed, but that he might cancel American support at the last minute if he felt that necessary.

While these signs from Washington were not very clear, it seems as if Washington was slowly accepting the need for getting rid of Diem, but wanted also to do the impossible—to seem not to be involved in it.

By early October the Washington policy seemed to be that the United States would not oppose a coup and would work with any new government that came about. At the same time Washington hoped that Diem would remain in power, and if the coup did take place, the United States did not want Diem to be killed.

In Saigon, Lodge felt that the coup was going to happen; things had moved too far and too fast to stop things now. On October 30, Lodge received a telegram from Washington telling him that the coup should not happen unless it was certain to succeed. Lodge reported back that there was nothing he could do to stop it. Whether that was true or not, the coup took place two days later on November 1, 1963. A CIA agent was at the headquarters of the generals with a direct phone line to the American Embassy. Lodge offered Diem and his family a plane to fly them out of the country. Diem refused the offer, and he and his brother went into hiding in the homes of friends.

A junta (joint ruling committee) consisting of Generals Minh, Kim and Dyon took control on November 1. The next day Diem and Nhu were captured and killed. Washington was shocked. Kennedy himself was deeply saddened and continued to talk about removing American forces from Vietnam. But nothing more than talks took place, for on November 22, 1963, in the streets of Dallas, Texas, John F. Kennedy was himself killed by an assassin's gun.

SEVEN

In Tonkin Gulf

The new president of the United States was Lyndon Baines Johnson. One of the best politicians since Franklin Roosevelt, Johnson had been poor as a child, but he had worked hard and had become the leader of the United States Senate, where his ability to bring opponents together and to make deals had made him a legend.

In 1960, Johnson sought the Democratic nomination for president. John F. Kennedy defeated him, but recognized that, as an Irish Catholic from the Northeast with a Harvard background, he needed help in winning the traditionally Democratic South. For that reason he selected Johnson to run for vice-president on his ticket. The two won a close race against Nixon and Lodge.

After the election Kennedy and his "New Frontiers-man" paid little attention to Johnson. Kennedy's people were very able and were very loyal to the president. Johnson, with his rough manner and folksy ways, was not liked by the Kennedy people. But he had his own vision for America. He wanted to bring about great changes—to complete the work of the man he idolized, Franklin Delano Roosevelt.

Johnson's presidency began in the tragedy of Dallas and was to end in the tragedy of Vietnam. His dream of a fair and wealthy society was left behind in the nightmare of war in a nation he may not have heard of in his youth. Johnson's skills were in domestic policy—social programs, justice, and civil rights—not foreign policy. But Johnson took over the nation's highest office at a time in history when a very important decision had to be made about foreign policy.

It was not really just one decision, though. No one came into the president's office and said, "Hey, you have to decide today if America is going to fight a war in Vietnam." No, what happened was that small decisions had to be made one at a time. Each one moved America closer to the day when it would wake up and find that it was at war. To gain a better understanding of what was to happen, let us step back a little and see what happened in Vietnam from the communist viewpoint.

In December of 1960, the National Liberation Front (NLF) was formed in South Vietnam. Its members included many parts of the Vietnamese community. There were communists, to be sure. In fact, the communists played a major role in the leadership of the NLF. But there were others, too, who sought a free and democratic Vietnam, who opposed the religious persecution of the Diem regime, who sought to overthrow the government if only to gain power for themselves.

There was something in the NLF to appeal to almost every part of Vietnamese society. In fact, by 1962, the NLF had become an important part of as many as eighty percent of the rural villages in South Vietnam. It had become a second government and one that was in many ways closer to the people.

It was also becoming pushier. With weapons from the North, it started a campaign against the village leaders appointed from Saigon. Hundreds of these were killed. The NLF killing in the villages, joined with Buddhist protests in the streets, made the government in Saigon a shaky one at best. Even without these problems, that government might have been in trouble, for Diem's death did nothing to end the battle for power among the politicians.

In January of 1964, just two months after Diem's death, the government in Saigon changed hands twice. It was to do so twelve more times in the next two years. The news, in short, was bad news for those who counted on the American-backed government in Saigon to hold off communism in Southeast Asia.

At this time the number of American advisors had grown to sixteen thousand—which is a good many "advisors" to have. Included in the advice they gave was a plan to have the South Vietnamese Navy act to cut off supplies from North Vietnam. Some of these supplies were being delivered by sea, landing on the coast of the

Gulf of Tonkin. The coastline of Vietnam is shaped like the letter "S", and the Gulf of Tonkin fills the upper loop in the letter.

Along this huge coastline the North Vietnamese could deliver their supplies almost anywhere, but, of course, there were only a few naval bases at which their ships could load. The easiest way to cut off naval shipments was to do so at their source—the North Vietnamese naval bases.

In January of 1964, the South Vietnamese Navy with the help of the CIA began firing at these bases from ships off shore. It was a small step to take, but an important one. South Vietnam's successes were to be American successes, and its failures were America's failures as well. The United States had raised the stakes just as the North Vietnamese had when they began supplying the NLF.

Within two months, the North Vietnamese raised the stakes again. NLF assaults expanded and included some attacks on Americans. The newest leaders of South Vietnam (General Minh and Tran Van Don) were not sure they would be able to contain the NLF. They began to talk of a "neutralist" answer. This would be similar to what happened in Laos. A government would be formed that included some NLF members in important positions, but the country would be neutral, at least for a while.

Secretary of Defense Robert McNamara was very much against a neutralist solution in Vietnam for he felt that it would simply mean a temporary neutralist government followed by an NLF takeover without the need to win a military victory. But the United States could not really oppose the wishes of the South Vietnamese leaders without offering them another solution, so the military commitment in South Vietnam was increased to twenty-three thousand advisors.

At the same time President Johnson ordered his aides to come up with a list of targets to be bombed in North Vietnam in case North Vietnam pushed too hard. Johnson's action here is important. The bombing of North Vietnam, a nation with no troops officially in South Vietnam, meant real war. It was also possible that the Chinese would come into such a war.

The action can be seen in different ways. It could be seen as though the United States was looking for an excuse to bomb North Vietnam or it could be seen as normal planning, just in case. In an age of jets and missiles, the leaders of a nation cannot be expected to think up their responses to attack after the attack has taken place. Things move too quickly for that. It is normal and proper that plans be developed in advance. The motto "Be Prepared" is not used only by the Boy Scouts.

As we will see the bombing plan probably fit somewhere between these two ideas. It was not exactly just a plan on a piece of paper nor was it the raising of a fist. It was more like taking off a glove, a decision that if the United States felt pushed there would be a strong response. This is the danger in contingency planning. The decision to take strong action against a country if it commits a certain act is easy to make if you do not believe that you will ever have to take the action. Then, when that country does act, the reaction takes place without much further thought. So a decision made without any belief that it will be needed becomes something close to a final decision.

By late spring little had changed. Indeed, if anything, matters were worse. The South Vietnamese, by this time led by General Khanh, asked the United States to help take the land war to North Vietnam. The request was turned down, but other choices were considered. Johnson himself was upset by the events in Southeast Asia. He asked the CIA to look into the reason given for American involvement: That the fall of South Vietnam would have a "domino" effect and lead to the toppling of other non-communist nations in Asia. The CIA disagreed with the theory.

Johnson apparently ignored the CIA's views, for, soon after its report, he took another quiet step in the growing conflict. The step had to be quiet because Johnson was beginning his campaign for election to a full term as president, and in that election he would paint his opponent, Senator Barry Goldwater, as a dangerous man who would readily risk war. He would try to show himself as a man of peace. No one would have believed Johnson's campaign if they knew of his next step. He was about to offer the North Vietnamese the choice of a carrot or a stick, and the stick was a very powerful one.

Johnson's messenger was Blair Seaborn, a Canadian diplomat, who had been recently assigned to the unpleasant post of being the Canadian delegate to the International Control Commission. That group, you remember, was set up by the Geneva agreements at the end of the French war. Its purpose was to oversee those agreements. The job was unpleasant because neither side had paid the least attention to the agreements for years. It was a do-nothing job, the kind that could place a diplomat out of the real action long enough so that everyone would forget about him.

As it turned out, Seaborn was to have an exciting and important role to play on his very first day on the job. The United States approached the Canadian government, which agreed to deliver a message through Seaborn to the government in Hanoi. In mid-June, Seaborn, armed with briefing papers from the American State Department, met with Pham Van Dong, the prime minister of North Vietnam.

The message he delivered was not very clear. He told the prime minister that while the United States had only slight interest in Vietnam, it also only had limited patience with the subversion sponsored by North Vietnam. On behalf of the United States he offered economic aid for North Vietnam in exchange for an agreement by that nation to halt its aid to the National Liberation Front.

Pham Van Dong's response was clearer. He told Seaborn that Hanoi was interested in a just solution to the problem. But that, for a solution to be just, it must include a neutralized South Vietnam, that is, a government including the NLF. Such a government would be seen as the first step toward making the nation one again. In general, this response was a rejection of the American carrot. But Phan Van Dong coupled it with a statement of interest in talks. In other words, he had heard what the Americans wanted and stated what the North Vietnamese wanted. Further talks might lead to a middle ground in which both sides got some part of what they wanted.

Seaborn warned him that, if pushed, the United States might feel obliged to carry the war into the north. The prime minister assured him that there would be no reason to do that and again stated his interest in further talks.

There were no further talks before trouble brewed, and there is no known record on paper as to why there were not. Seaborn, an experienced diplomat, felt that the North Vietnamese were serious and looked forward to further discussions, but the State Department did not follow up on his offer to start such talks. In eight more weeks it would be too late for talking.

Richard Nixon has said that the greatest danger to peace is miscalculation: one side misunderstanding the other side. In this case it seems likely that both sides miscalculated. The North Vietnamese were not told what the American "stick" was, because Seaborn himself did not know that President Johnson had agreed to a program of air and naval bombing of the north if they did not stop aiding the NLF. It is possible they thought the American "stick" was something else: an increase in military advisors or arms shipments to South Vietnam. These matters would not have troubled them very much.

It seems sure that the United States was wrong about the dedication of the North Vietnamese and their willingness to suffer great losses to reach their goal of a united Vietnam under communist rule. We will never know if a knowledge of those facts would have made any difference. The situation in South Vietnam was so bad that it might not have.

Secretary of Defense Robert McNamara believed

forty percent of South Vietnam was under NLF control or influence and that the South Vietnamese had very little will to fight back. The soldiers were deserting, and the people's support for the war was very low. The American presence was disliked by many.

In that same report to President Johnson, McNamara stated: "We are not acting against North Vietnam except by a very modest 'covert' program operated by South Vietnam . . . a program so limited it is unlikely to have any significant effect."

The "very modest" program mentioned by McNamara was Operation 34-A, and it was going to have a very important effect. South Vietnamese gunboats, under directions from American commanders, were bombarding islands used as bases by the North Vietnamese along the Gulf of Tonkin. Late on the evening of July 31, 1964, a group of such boats left Da Nang to engage in such a mission well into North Vietnamese territory.

At the same time the American destroyer USS *Maddox* was sailing in international waters one hundred miles to the south. Its orders were to come not closer than eight miles from the coast. By noon on August 2, 1964, the *Maddox* was in the general area in which the South Vietnamese had been bombarding when it came under fire from three North Vietnamese torpedo boats. The *Maddox* reported the attack to the Pentagon and forced the attackers to retreat. It reported its position as thirty miles offshore. President Johnson ordered another destroyer to join the *Maddox*. The second ship—the USS *C. Turner Joy*—joined the *Maddox* in the early morning of August 4. At about the same time, further Operation

34-A attacks were launched against North Vietnamese facilities on the coast, and South Vietnamese planes attacked North Vietnamese border villages.

A few hours later the *Maddox* and the *C. Turner Joy* reported a second attack. Later telegrams from the ships were less clear as to whether an attack had taken place or not. But it does seem clear that the president and his advisors believed that a second attack had taken place and had good reasons for that belief. The president ordered the bombing of selected targets in North Vietnam and announced his decision to the American people as the planes were returning from their mission. They had destroyed twenty-five North Vietnamese patrol vessels and a large number of oil storage tanks.

The Gulf of Tonkin incident was the beginning of a full-scale American commitment to the war in Vietnam. It is the major event of the period and, as we shall see, provided the legal basis for further American involvement. But what happened and why it happened remains unclear.

An attack of some sort took place. It seems safe to believe that the attack took place because of the South Vietnamese coastal raids as well as the bombing of the border villages. What is not clear is whether the second attack, which led to the American bombing, really took place and why the *Maddox* was in the area to begin with.

All that is officially said about the *Maddox* is that it was on a regular information gathering mission. If that mission was meant to aid the Operation 34-A attacks, then one can understand, from a military sense, why the North Vietnamese responded to those attacks by attacks on American vessels. But Operation 34-A had been going on for six months when the Gulf of Tonkin incident took place, and the North Vietnamese had not attacked American vessels before.

The North Vietnamese response seemed well prepared. Coming as it did so soon after the Seaborn mission to Hanoi, it is best understood by assuming that the North Vietnamese were testing to see what the American "stick" might be. It is also likely that the North Vietnamese were simply angry with the Operation 34-A attacks and were showing the Americans that they would be held responsible for future ones.

Whatever the reason, the Gulf of Tonkin incident was to lead to hundreds of thousands of deaths and eight more years of war.

For some months, as we know, there had been plans to deal with an attack by the North Vietnamese. One part of those plans was to get an agreement from the Congress giving the president the power to act freely in Vietnam. President Johnson had spent many years in Congress. He was an expert at getting what he wanted from it, but he knew also that he had to respect its authority. Under the Constitution of the United States only Congress may declare war.

Johnson did not want a declaration of war because that act carried with it the danger that the Russians and the Chinese would become obligated by treaty to declare war on the United States. While that was unlikely, the danger of it was too great to risk.

The resolution drafted by Johnson's aides was not a declaration of war, but its language provided a legal basis for almost any action that the president chose to take. After talking with Congressional leaders, the resolution, known as the Gulf of Tonkin Resolution, was presented to Congress and passed by both the House of Representatives and the Senate on August 7, 1964. The vote in the House was 416–0, and the vote in the Senate was 88–2. The two Senators opposing the resolution were Wayne Morse of Oregon and Ernest Gruening of Alaska. Both felt that the resolution gave the president too much power. Both were right.

The important language read as follows:

Resolved by the Senate and House of Representatives of the United States of America in Congress assembled, that the Congress approve and support the determination of the President, as Commander in Chief, to take all necessary measures to repel any armed attack and to prevent further aggression.

The formal language is amazing in its scope. The Congress gave the president the power to "take all necessary measures" to "prevent further aggression." What measures were necessary? What actions could be seen as aggression? These were matters for the president to decide.

The resolution was passed on promises from Secretary McNamara and Secretary Rusk that the United States had not acted against the North Vietnamese. Included in these promises were statements from both men that the South Vietnamese coastal raids were conducted in the south. Secretary McNamara admitted that he thought they may have included some raids on the north. This hesitation about the area of the raids is odd because McNamara had received papers on the subject on May 19, June 13, July 1 and July 28.

Had Congress been fully aware of the nature of the raids, it is unlikely that the outcome would have been much different. A very popular president, who was running for reelection, had asked a Congress controlled by his fellow Democrats for the power to act in response to a foreign attack on American ships in international waters. Most of the Congress was up for reelection, too, and the public would have been very angered by a vote against the resolution.

Whether they knew it or not, and many said later that they did not, the Congress had given the president the power to wage war in Southeast Asia and over the months and years ahead, the president would use that power fully.

As much as anything else, Vietnam involved a conflict between Western technology and Eastern patience. In the upper photo, an American helicopter carries one of dozens of trucks off a freighter. In the lower photo, a group of Viet Cong load ammunition by hand.

An American fire base is shown from the air in the upper photo. In the lower picture, one of its powerful artillery pieces is readied for firing.

Warfare in Vietman was not confined to the battlefield and not all warriors wore uniforms. The top photo shows the remains of an automobile used in a Viet Cong terrorist bombing in Saigon. The bottom photo depicts two suspected Viet Cong terrorists being taken away for questioning.

One machine gunner rests between attacks while another sets off on a night mission.

EIGHT

Thunder and Lightning

For America, the war in Vietnam had begun. At home very few people noticed this. The country was torn between the news of a presidential election campaign and worry about the battle for the rights of American minorities, in which young Americans would give their lives in a situation that was truly black and white. The Vietnam war was only a cloud on the horizon. But that cloud was to bring a thunder without equal in the history of warfare—Operation Rolling Thunder, the air war against North Vietnam.

At first, the American policy was to be one of increasing pressure to force the North Vietnamese to stop their support for rebellion in the south. To avoid miscalculation, or further miscalculation, President Johnson sent another message to Hanoi through Blair Seaborn. Seaborn informed Pham Van Dong that the United States would take the war more and more to the north. The prime minister reacted with great anger and with the threat to spread the war through all of Southeast Asia.

But the United States bombardment and the threats of stronger action ahead did nothing to help the military or political situation in the south. Between mid-August and mid-September, the leadership in Saigon changed hands five more times between Generals Minh and Khanh. At the end of August, nearly five hundred persons were killed in religious rioting in the South Vietnamese capital.

This time, though, the protests were not limited to Saigon. The first antiwar demonstrations on an American college campus took place at the University of California in Berkeley on September 30, and a number of important people in the United States began to speak about their doubts as to the wisdom of American involvement. Among these people were Senator William Fulbright, the chief sponsor of the Tonkin Gulf Resolution, and Robert Kennedy, President Kennedy's brother and Lyndon Johnson's Attorney General.

Just at the time that some Americans began to be worried by their nation's role in Vietnam, the war came home to America in a very dramatic way. On November 1, NLF forces attacked the United States Air Force base at Bien Hoa. Four Americans were killed and five bombers were destroyed. These were not the first Americans to die in Vietnam, but the ones who had died before had not been attacked because they were Americans. They had been killed while they were advising

South Vietnamese troops. This was an attack on United States forces because they were just that. The American Joint Chiefs of Staff described the attack to the president as "a change in the ground rules." They asked for permission to bomb North Vietnamese Air Force bases.

The president was only two days away from an election, and he refused to take immediate action. He asked instead that the State Department prepare a list of choices for him. On November 3, 1964 Lyndon Johnson defeated Barry Goldwater by a huge number of votes. Three weeks later he was presented with the State Department's list of choices.

The choice selected was that of a "surgical" bombing. Targets would be selected and destroyed; then the bombing would stop while a North Vietnamese response was awaited. If no acceptable response was received, a second round of bombing would begin. Again the bombers would stop. The State Department thought that the North Vietnamese would seek talks within two to six months.

While Johnson picked the surgical bombing, he did not start it at once. He would wait for another North Vietnamese action. As the important year of 1964 came to an end, there was another change in the Saigon government. Nguyen Cao Ky and Nguyen Van Thieu were part of the new government. They were to stay in power in one job or another until the very last days of the war. This political calm gave the South Vietnamese the ability to continue their struggle.

By early 1965, this was clearly a war against North Vietnam. While there certainly had been some North

Vietnamese troops in South Vietnam prior to the Gulf of Tonkin incident, they had played a quiet role. North Vietnamese troops now fought in the South in the open and with great skill. Their presence caused more American planning, but this time those plans called for the use of American ground troops.

The NLF pushed again on February 7, 1965, when they attacked the American military base at Pleiku. Nine Americans died and seventy-six were wounded. President Johnson ordered an immediate response. Operation Flaming Dart involved fifty planes from American aircraft carriers. Together they attacked a major North Vietnamese base at Dong Hoi. Because of the way the war was changing, President Johnson ordered the families of American troops out of Vietnam.

Three days later the NLF attacked a hotel being used as barracks by American soldiers. President Johnson decided that the policy of responding when attacked was not leading anywhere and started a new policy of "sustained reprisal." This strange phrase really meant a policy of bombing-until-they-stop. No attack would be needed in the future. Day after day, week after week, the bombers would fly over North Vietnam. Operation Rolling Thunder had begun. It was to last for three and a half years and to have almost no real effect.

While this type of bombing makes military sense because it can cause great damage with a very low risk to the pilots and planes, it has not been a very successful strategy. The Germans tried it against the British in World War II, and it backfired on them because it made the British fight harder. The British and Americans tried it against Germany later in the war with more success because they were able to destroy much of Germany's war industries. The Americans also tried the tactic on the Japanese in World War II and accomplished very little until atomic weapons were used.

There was every reason to believe that the plan would be far less successful against the North Vietnamese. That nation did not have the many large cities and industrial areas that Germany had, so there were no very important targets. Most of North Vietnam's supplies could be brought in from China along trails American bombers could not find. The supply depots could easily be spread throughout the countryside. When you spread out the targets the bombing becomes more difficult.

But, in March of 1965, Rolling Thunder began, and behind it came American Marines who landed at the naval base in Da Nang. They had been sent to Vietnam against the wishes of Ambassador Taylor. He felt that American troops would never succeed in a guerrilla war in Asia. They would always be targets, but would never be able to tell who among the natives was the enemy until the first shots had been fired.

On March 8, three thousand five hundred marines landed. By June there were fifty-one thousand foreign troops in South Vietnam. Most of these were Americans, but some seven thousand were from New Zealand and Australia, who were part of the SEATO alliance.

At first these troops were not meant to fight. Their job was to aid the South Vietnamese army, not to oppose the NLF and North Vietnamese themselves. But they were allowed to defend themselves against enemy attacks.

Naturally, such a large number of troops traveling with South Vietnamese army troops who were looking for combat would have many opportunities to defend themselves when fights broke out. The idea of just advising the South Vietnamese was a fiction, and in April, 1965, it ended when the President allowed United States ground troops to take offensive action against NLF and North Vietnamese troops in South Vietnam.

But, for the moment, the major American involvement was in the air. By June, 1965, Operation Rolling Thunder had earned its name. American bombers were making four thousand eight hundred attacks a month on North Vietnamese targets. By 1967, that number would reach twelve thousand. By the time Rolling Thunder ended in October of 1968, more bombs had been dropped on North Vietnam than had been dropped in all of World War II.

The days of major ground war were not far off though. The air war was not having any noticeable effect on the situation in South Vietnam. Its main target was supplies, and the guerrillas could do without new supplies for long periods of time. In July, President Johnson raised the American commitment to one hundred and twenty-five thousand troops and announced that it was likely that more would be needed.

The first ground combat operations began a new era in the history of warfare. Small groups of troops were brought to an area by helicopters. There they sought out enemy forces and fought those that they found. When the fight was over, the helicopters would come back and return the American troops to their home base and take the wounded to hospitals. No land was gained nor was any land really wanted. This was not a war for land. It was a war in which both sides sought to cause enough losses on the other side to make them give up hope. Two armies were engaged in a siege against each other, trying to wear each other down.

A part of this awful business was the body count. Each day military officers in Saigon would tell the press the number of enemy killed. These numbers came from reports from the field, and each day on American television a report would be given on the number of enemy dead. This would always be a fairly large number while the number of American dead would always be a fairly small number.

But that number of American dead was growing quickly as the United States combat role increased. Between August and December of 1965, 808 Americans were killed in Vietnam. In the next year the total reached over five thousand. General Westmoreland was told by McNamara that he could ask for as many troops as he needed. And he needed greater and greater numbers because, among other reasons, the South Vietnamese army was not fighting very well.

One cause of this can be found in these figures. Of those called into the South Vietnamese army only one out of seven showed up. Almost one out of every four South Vietnamese troops deserted. For cultural, religious and political reasons, the people of South Vietnam were not strongly in support of the war.

The chances of defeating an enemy like the NLF, who could melt into the villages at a moment's notice, were very slight without support among the people for their defeat.

The problem of support for the war was not only in South Vietnam. Opposition in the United States also was growing quickly. In November of 1965, two Americans imitated the Buddhist monks and burned themselves on American streets. Those same streets were filled by thirty-five thousand protesters who marched on the White House that same month.

The roots of the American protest movement are many. At first it was a radical movement, led by Americans who, for one reason or another, rejected the society in which they lived. Some of these people had been working for racial equality in the United States and had been turned against their own society by the horror they saw in some communities' efforts to keep black citizens in a poor position. Others had chosen a radical form of politics in which they saw the Chinese or Russian communist system as better than the American capitalist system. Still others were pacifists who opposed any war.

These people were very sincere. But it is fair to say that the first protesters had no real influence or popular support. It was not until 1968, when the antiwar movement had found leadership in elected officials from the American Midwest, that it began to have a real effect on American policy.

Yet these first protests brought national attention to the events in Southeast Asia. The slow growth of the war had not been noticed in the mid-1960s. These were dramatic times. The civil rights movement was making progress and making changes all over the nation. The

American economy was booming and Lyndon Johnson was building the Great Society he had promised in his election campaign.

Vietnam was first noticed by young men who were being drafted into the army. College students, faced with two years in the military, listened to those who said that the Vietnam war was wasting lives. It was their lives that would be wasted.

The students began to ask basic questions. Why are we in Vietnam? Was the NLF a nationalist or a communist organization? Would the fall of Vietnam mean the fall of all of Southeast Asia? If Vietnam is important to the free world, does that mean that the very unfree South Vietnamese government should be helped by American weapons and American lives?

The government did not answer these questions very well. Facts about America's role were first denied and then explained away. The Johnson Administration was not believed by an important part of the American people. The antiwar groups also could not always be believed. Some seemed to make heroes of the NLF. While it is true that the NLF came closer to meeting the hopes of the South Vietnamese people than did their government, they also could be very cruel and not necessarily people to look up to. Between 1966 and 1971, NLF forces had killed over twenty thousand civilians and kidnapped many more. These were not acts of war, but part of a campaign of terrorism.

Despite growing doubts and active opposition at home, the war in Vietnam continued to grow. By the end of 1965, there were one hundred and eighty-one thousand

American troops in Vietnam. By the end of 1966, that figure had reached three hundred and eighty-five thousand. The next year the figure jumped by another one hundred thousand and by the end of 1968 it had reached its greatest strength of five hundred and thirty-six thousand. The casualties grew along with the troop figures. Casualties (dead or wounded) rose from eighteen thousand in 1966 to nearly fifty thousand in 1968.

These are just numbers, and they do not explain the lives and deaths of American troops in Vietnam. These young people found themselves in the middle of a war that they did not understand, following orders that often made little sense and returning home to an America that either ignored them or disliked them.

The story of these American troops is a complex one, which continues to the present day. In the next chapter we will try to get some feeling of how they viewed the war, America's attitude toward them and their role in it.

NINE

Over There

Every war is different. Each is fought in different ways and does different things to the people who fought in it. One way of learning about a war is through the music and writing that comes out of it. In these things we show our feelings very clearly.

There were only three songs about the war in Vietnam that became popular, even though most record buyers were the same young people most affected by the war.

The first song was about serving in the Green Berets, a special group of troops whose training was thought to make them very good anti-guerrilla forces. The second song was an antiwar song, which placed the blame for all war on the fact that soldiers did not refuse to fight. The third song that was popular, long after the war was over, leaves a picture of young Americans eager to fight, who are faced with an enemy as good as they are in a war that is very hard to understand. In the end, the young soldiers lie in fear at night or seek escape from the fear in drugs or music.

Compare these songs with the patriotic songs of every other American war. The hopefulness is gone after the Green Berets prove to be no magic solution to jungle warfare. It is replaced with a feeling of dislike for all war, and finally by a song that tells about the changes this strange war made in the lives of individual solders.

It is this last idea that may remain the longest. While other wars have led to great novels and many histories, most of the few books written about Vietnam have been the stories of ordinary soldiers, histories telling the sad and funny tales of war; showing the courage and cruelty of men in combat. Much of what these books say is horrible. Cruelty is probably always a part of war. The difference between Vietnam and other wars is that the soldiers were willing to tell what they did, both good and bad, and the effects that the war had on them.

The books and the music show, from the American side, a very personal war. While many Americans felt that they were fighting a war that had some good purpose, many others came to hate it and its purposes. There was no cheering in the barracks (or on the homefront) when an important battle was won. There was no feeling of brotherhood.

Some people feel that all of this says something about Americans of the 1960s and 1970s. They say that they were somehow softer than their parents, not hardened

by the cruel economic Depression during which most of
their parents had grown up. They say that the war was
strange because the soldiers were strange.

Others believe that the war itself was strange and
that its strangeness caused changes in those who fought
in it. If you look at the time starting from the inauguration of Richard Nixon, you can see their point.

Nixon was elected president in part because of a campaign promise to "Vietnamize" the war. That is, he intended to replace American troops with Vietnamese
troops. It became clear, though, that Nixon saw this as
a slow process. Americans would start pulling out in large
numbers only after the North Vietnamese had started to
do some pulling out of their own.

To the newest private in the American army this meant
that he was going into combat only to wear down the
North Vietnamese until they were ready to agree to a
settlement. It is not surprising to find out that no one
was looking for the honor of being the last American
to die in Vietnam.

This fact and other facts about the Vietnam "War"
are important to understand. The average soldier served
for twelve months with one month's vacation. In every
twelve-month period a whole new American army came
in and learned the lessons that the earlier army had
learned and then moved out again to be replaced by a
new group of fresh troops. These were short-term troops
committed to a short-term war. Their lives were not
protected by winning battles that would weaken their
enemy. Their lives were protected by keeping low for a
year.

Only a small part of these forces (ten percent) were combat troops. The other ninety percent were troops in charge of supplies, bookkeeping, plane and tank mechanics and a thousand other housekeeping chores.

A very large percent were officers (fifteen percent). In World War II, only about eight percent of troops were officers. These officers served even shorter periods than the regular soldiers, and so the leaders often had less experience in war than the men who were supposed to follow them. And the followers were young, very young. In World War II the average age of a soldier was twenty-six. In Vietnam the average age was nineteen. In part, the young age can be explained by the draft system.

The draft was the way in which most of these young men found their way into the army. (The other branches of the armed forces had a higher percentage of volunteers.) At the age óf eighteen, every American male was required to go to his local draft board (located in his town or in a neighboring community) and to register for the draft. Once a month the Selective Service System in Washington would tell each local draft board how many men they had to call in for the month. The local boards were made up of private citizens volunteering their services. These boards would then go through their list of men with a classification of 1-A and tell them to take a medical exam. Those who were classified as 1-A and passed the medical would be taken into the armed services until the month's quota had been reached.

The classification of 1-A meant that one had no "deferment" (excuse). Deferments were available at first on a number of grounds: working in a defense industry,

having a family and going to college. During the war
one guess is that fifteen million young men got out of
the draft through the deferment system. Most of these
had student deferments.

The student deferment system was so widely used that
a young man who had finished high school, reached the
age of eighteen, had not entered college and had no
serious medical problems was sure to be drafted right
away. Thus, a large number of eighteen-year-olds were
drafted every month, keeping the average age of a soldier
low. The short term of service in Vietnam also kept the
age down, since the new troops brought in would be
picked from among the new draftees. The system was
deeply disliked for two very different reasons.

First, many people felt that the system was unfair to
poor families, who were often minorities. Their sons
lacked the money or education to attend college, so
instead they would fight the nation's war while the sons
of the wealthier Americans stayed safe at school.

Of course, college ends one way or another, but
college graduates could get into officer-training programs
or had the typing and bookkeeping skills needed to get a
safe office job.

The result was that twenty-eight percent of all the
combat troops in Vietnam were black. That is nearly
three times the number one would expect since, at the
time, blacks were only about ten percent of the population. Thus this system favored the rich over the poor and
the white over the black.

But many white college students also disliked the draft
system. Their reason was very different. The draft was

the living symbol of the war. It was a part of the war that was in every community and could be opposed by individuals opposed to the war.

Hundreds of thousands of young men decided not to register for the draft. Not all of these disagreed with the war. Many did though, and twenty-five thousand faced criminal charges during this period. Of these, more than three thousand two hundred went to prison. Tens of thousands of others moved to Canada or to Sweden to avoid being drafted into the armed services.

Some part of the resistance to the draft was caused by religious beliefs. Such cases were very difficult. Any person could say that their religious beliefs stopped them from fighting in the war. The local draft board had to decide whether that claim was sincere or was based instead on something else: politics or a simple desire not to fight.

Those who the boards found to have real religious beliefs against military action were made to either serve in the army in a position such as a medic, or to perform other service as a civilian. These other jobs often were in hospitals or other public agencies.

Much of the unfairness of the draft ended in 1969 when President Nixon announced the end of college deferments. The local board selection systems were also replaced with a lottery in which a number was drawn for each date in the year. Those whose birthdate had the lowest number would be called first.

The end of the college deferments brought about a wider opposition to the war on college campuses, for now all students had a real interest in the war. This is not to say that the students were afraid of fighting. Rather, the fact that they, too, stood a chance of having their lives changed led to more interest in the thing that would cause the change.

The start of 1969 saw several things come together to make the Vietnam experience even more tragic than it had already been. There were half a million very young Americans in uniform in a foreign land. They were there to fight in a war that their nation's leader had decided should not be fought by Americans. They were hearing from all sides that the war was a waste, that no one should be fighting it. They also heard that the military was being held back and, if left alone, could end the war in a few months. There were no great rallies. There were no parades sending them off or greeting them when they returned. The nation had become turned off by the war that they were going off to fight.

The American troops did not feel very much like fighting.

Before 1969, the number of American troops who ran away from the army had been lower than in World War II or the Korean War. By 1971, the rate had jumped four hundred percent. Out of every one thousand troops, seventy-five deserted. But desertion means an unexcused absence beyond thirty days. Shorter absences went under the initials A.W.O.L. (absent without official leave). The AWOL rate was one hundred and seventy-five out of one thousand. When the numbers are combined, they reach two hundred and fifty out of one thousand. One-fourth of the troops walked away from their jobs for some period of time.

Desertion was not the only problem that low spirits brought with it. Drugs were easily available in Southeast Asia at much lower prices than in the United States. To the frightened, the confused, or the bored, drugs provided one means of getting away. One study says that drug use among American troops climbed from twenty-nine percent in 1969 to fifty-eight percent in 1971. Heroin use in that time climbed from an estimated two percent to twenty-two percent. In 1971, four times as many American troops were treated for drug problems than were treated for war wounds.

As we have seen, no one wanted to be the last American to die in Southeast Asia. Officers who ordered troops into dangerous combat areas or were otherwise seen as 'gung ho" found themselves in danger from their own troops. The term "fragging" was derived from the use of fragmentation grenades (hand grenades that broke up into small pieces when exploded) to kill officers in their sleep. Such things were widely reported. No one will ever know how many officers were killed by their own troops in the field. There, the death could easily be blamed on enemy action. It is known, though, that between 1969 and 1971 more than seven hundred grenade attempts were made on officers' lives and that more than eighty deaths took place.

This was an army that could not possibly fight a war. Young and inexperienced troops, many of whom were using drugs at least some of the time, were led by inexperienced officers who could not command their troops for fear of being killed. Together, their mission was to keep the heat on long enough so that the president could get some concession from the North Vietnamese and then withdraw them with "honor."

They came home bitter and confused. Many of them formed antiwar groups of their own. But these were not based on the political ideas that the college students relied on. Their opposition was based on their own experiences; on what they saw as a waste of their lives and the lives of their friends.

And they were coming home to small towns all over America. There in Middle America they did not form committees or march on the Capital. But they talked and few were happy about what they had been through. In those days, when Middle America gave up on the war, the nation wrote off Vietnam as a bad experience, something that we probably should not have gotten into and certainly should be out of.

In doing so, though, there was risk of writing off those who had chosen or been chosen to fight and die in Vietnam. They had been to a place that no one wanted to talk about, so no one wanted to talk to them. Vietnam was something that America wanted to forget about, and in doing so, it forgot hundreds of thousands of its own children, grown to manhood in a foreign land filled with violence and pain.

TEN

1968

The year 1968 was the most important in the ten years of American involvement in Vietnam. It is also among the most important in the two hundred years of American history. These two facts are connected. Major events in Vietnam were to have a lasting effect on American history and major events in the United States were to have a similar effect on the struggle in Southeast Asia. By the end of the year America was as ruined emotionally as Vietnam was physically. One of the major American political figures of the century was out of office and another had made a comeback. Two other important Americans were dead from violence and, though very few knew it yet, hundreds of Vietnamese villagers had been deliberately slaughtered by American soldiers.

In order to clearly see what went on in 1968 we should go back a few months.

By the middle of 1967, it was clear to some, at least, that the bombings were not having much effect. You recall that the original guess had been that the North Vietnamese would seek peace within six months. More than two years of bombing had taken place, but no change in the North Vietnamese position was seen. So the long-range goal of the bombing—peace negotiations —had not been reached. Neither had the short-term goal —reduction of supplies to the antigovernment forces in the south.

Many of these supplies came down from the north along what was known as the Ho Chi Minh Trail. This was a network of roads along the Laotian side of the Vietnam-Laos border. The bombing targeted the main roadway, which was some three thousand miles long, but with its side paths and detours, the trail itself was actually over eight thousand miles of roads. To keep their forces in the south supplied, the Vietnamese only needed to move sixty tons of material every day along this network. Twenty small trucks would do the job.

It is easy to see that the chances of spotting and bombing twenty camouflaged trucks among thousands of miles of roadway would not be an easy one. The trucks moved at night and hid in the jungle during the day. Troops coming from the north were also safe from the bombers because they moved in small groups and could easily hide themselves from high-flying airplanes. One could hope to damage the trail so that nothing could move on it, but every night thousands of Vietnamese went out to repair the day's damage.

There was one old-fashioned way to deal with the problem and one very new one. The old-fashioned way was to send troops to take and hold the Trail, but it was located in Laos, a neutral country, and President Johnson refused to send troops into that country. The more modern approach was soon given the name of "Mc-Namara's Fence."

This was a system of microphones, disguised as plants and other natural objects, which were dropped along the trail from planes. These would pick up the sounds of troops or trucks and signal the bombers as to where and when they should attack. But in order to keep the microphones in place, they needed to be surrounded by mines, which would stop their removal. Mine crews came under attack from North Vietnamese troops and the system never really worked.

After the failure of the bombing and the fence, Secretary McNamara apparently became increasingly worried about the war. He sent the president memoranda suggesting that the bombing was a failure and was taking too many innocent lives. Johnson offered to stop the bombing in exchange for peace negotiations. The North Vietnamese refused. In November of 1967, Secretary McNamara resigned.

The American public knew little of what was going on. They knew that there were many American troops in South Vietnam and that bombers were dropping hundreds of tons of explosives every day. They heard of fighting here and there, and they were given the idea that the war was ending. They strongly supported the war in public opinion polls, and while there were demonstrations against the war, there were many rallies in favor of it as well.

The nation as a whole supported the war effort and scorned the protestors. But this support was based on faith, on a trust in the national leadership, and on a belief that the war was not only for a good purpose but that the goal could be reached. The next few months would seriously strain that faith if not break it entirely. When those months were over, more Americans would support the war than would oppose it, but their support was very slight.

It began on January 21, 1968, at a place called Khe Sanh just a few miles south of the line dividing North and South Vietnam and even closer to the Laotian border. A small plateau and a few surounding hills were held by over five thousand American marines and South Vietnamese troops. It was not a very important place, but it was a place where the North Vietnamese might be drawn into a serious battle. In that way it was much like Dien Bien Phu, but in other ways it was just the opposite. Dien Bien Phu was a valley, and the French lost there because they did not hold the high ground surrounding their troops. At Khe Sanh the Americans and South Vietnamese held the high ground.

At Dien Bien Phu the French were shocked at the size of the force opposing them. At Khe Sanh the microphones prepared for "McNamara Fence" gave the warning that a large number of North Vietnamese were moving into the area. At Dien Bien Phu, the loss of the airfields had doomed the defenders. At Khe Sanh the airfield was better protected, and even if lost, the troops could still be supplied by helicopter. At Dien Bien Phu the French had little help from the outside. At Khe Sanh the North Vietnamese faced five thousand bombs a day in an area the size of a small town. Imagine ten square miles near where you live, then think about what it would be like if five thousand bombs fell on that area every day.

There was another difference between the two situations—the most important difference of all—television. Khe Sanh was attacked for seventy-seven days and during that time reporters and television crews were brought in and out. Every night the American news programs showed the fighting and showed the fighters. These familiar American faces were set against a strange and foreign background. They were fighting an enemy that the American people believed to be near defeat, and they were in trouble.

Comparisons with the French at Dien Bien Phu were sure to be made. The comparison is almost silly because of the enormous advantages the Americans had over the French, but they were made anyway. The nightly drama began to make many Americans nervous about the war effort. Many were concerned that not enough forces were being committed. Many others began to wonder if further commitment was worthwhile. Then, just ten days after the drama at Khe Sanh had begun, the same news programs showed a far more sudden and far more disturbing event.

Tet is the New Year celebration in Vietnam. It is both a holiday and a holy day. Every year cease-fires had been declared around the time of Tet. This year was no exception. Despite reports of troop movements in South

Vietnam, half of the South Vietnamese Army went home for vacation and the general appearance was one of rest.

That rest was broken on January 31, when eighty thousand NLF and North Vietnamese troops began a simultaneous attack on nearly every community of any size in South Vietnam. That night the television news showed marines defending the United States Embassy in Saigon.

How could such a thing have happened in a war that Americans thought was being won?

The "how" was simple and showed the basic weakness of the American military position in Vietnam. Tens of thousands of NLF and North Vietnamese troops put on normal clothes and gathered in communities throughout the South. There they grouped, armed, and changed into uniforms. Then, at a certain time, they attacked their targets. Up until the point that they showed themselves in uniform and armed, there was nothing to stop them.

Their attacks were not successful. In fact, the Tet offensive can be described as a major military defeat. Though two thousand five hundred American troops died during the attacks, many times that number of North Vietnamese forces were killed and no important goal was taken.

While Tet was a great military defeat for the North Vietnamese, it was also a major political victory. At about the same time as the Tet offensive was ending, so was the siege of Khe Sanh. There, too, the Americans and South Vietnamese were victorious, but, after the siege was lifted, the position at Khe Sanh was no longer important.

Tet and Khe Sanh left Americans with major questions. Could this enemy be defeated? If so, for what purpose? Why fight for a place for eleven weeks when the place had no real importance? How there could be an end to a war where the soliders could disappear into any village at night? These questions were being asked in the middle of a presidential election campaign.

Lyndon Johnson was running again, but despite his enormous victory in 1964, he had strong opposition from inside his own party. Senator Engene McCarthy of Minnesota challenged Johnson on the war issue. McCarthy was an unusual man. A poet and former monk, he gave an impression of complete peace. This made him an odd choice to lead a movement that was as passionate as any in recent years. But McCarthy was effective in getting support from college students, and they formed an important campaign force with ability and with time to spare. On March 12, the first primary election was held, as always, in the state of New Hampshire. McCarthy lost, but only by a small margin, this in New Hampshire, a state as conservative as any in the nation.

The nation was shaken but not as badly as it soon would be. *The New York Times* soon carried two stories that must have been leaked by someone in the government. The stories said that General Westmoreland had requested two hundred thousand more troops and that Johnson had ordered thirty thousand more Americans to Vietnam. A few days later, Robert F. Kennedy entered the race for the Democratic nomination.

Eugene McCarthy was one thing, but Robert Kennedy was something very different. McCarthy could count on very little support from Democratic party officials. Kennedy, by now a Senator from New York, could count on wide support from such people. He was also popular among working people. At the 1964 Democratic convention, which nominated Lyndon Johnson, Kennedy was supposed to introduce a film on his late brother. Johnson, fearing that people would turn to Kennedy, set the speech for after the nomination. When Kennedy spoke, Johnson's fears were justified. The clapping lasted for twenty minutes; the feeling probably lasted much longer.

Kennedy's entry meant that Lyndon Johnson would have to campaign very hard to gain his own party's nomination while running the nation and fighting a war. On March 31, Johnson spoke to the nation on television. He announced a freeze in the number of troops in Vietnam, a cutback in the bombing and, in a brief and shocking announcement, he told the country that he would no longer be a candidate for renomination.

Four days later the nation received another shock. Dr. Martin Luther King, civil rights leader and winner of the Nobel Peace prize, was killed by an assassin's bullet. The nation's cities broke out in rioting. Dr. King was a symbol of peaceful struggle, and it is terrible to know that he died by violent means and that his death set off a great wave of violence and property destruction.

Just as the Tet offensive ended the idea that the war in Vietnam was ending, so did Dr. King's death end the idea that the long civil rights struggle at home was nearing its end. The violence of war on the television screens and rioting in the cities of America created great divisions in the nation.

Young and old, black and white, cities and countryside

seemed to be split in ways that would not heal. Even the antiwar movement was split. There were those who believed in the normal political processes and those who believed in violence. There were those who saw the movement as a way to end a war that seemed to be against basic American values. Others saw the movement as a way to gain a complete change in American society.

The movement was split, too, by the Kennedy candidacy. Some decided to stay with McCarthy because he had been the first to take a stand. Others switched to Kennedy because they believed he was more able or because they believed he could be elected. Lyndon Johnson's vice-president, the very respected Hubert Humphrey, also entered the campaign, and the race looked like a close one.

The last major primary was in California on June 6. Kennedy won and seemed to be heading into the August convention as the favorite when, after speaking to his campaign workers, he, like his brother and Dr. King, was killed by a bullet fired from a gun by a fanatic.

The nation mourned its second Kennedy in five years, and the race for the Democratic nomination was a wreck. Whatever strength McCarthy had had, had been lost to Kennedy. Hubert Humphrey had closer ties to the Democratic leaders, and he had the support of Lyndon Johnson, but the antiwar groups were coming to Chicago to make their presence felt.

The Republicans had no such problems. They were to nominate Richard Nixon with ease. For the fourth time in sixteen years, Nixon would be on the Republican ticket. Like any Republican candidate, he had almost no

chance against a united Democratic Party. The number
of Democratic voters in the United States is greater than
the Republican, and more independents voted Democratic than Republican in most presidential elections. But
Richard Nixon was not to face a united Democratic
party. He was to face one that was broken apart, for the
convention in Chicago had turned into what a federal
commission later called a police riot.

Many antiwar protesters had come to Chicago just to
protest against the war. Others had come looking for a
fight. Democrats ran Chicago and their leader was Mayor
Richard Daley. Daley ran the city as though it were a
kingdom. He would not allow a group of long-haired
college students to disrupt the Democratic convention
in his city.

There were more police and National Guard troops
than demonstrators. When the protesters marched toward the convention hall, a bloody battle broke out,
which the demonstrators were certain to lose. Hundreds
were injured and millions more watched the struggle on
television and heard it condemned on the convention
floor.

Hubert Humphrey was nominated to lead the Democratic Party in the fall election, but there was almost no
Democratic Party to lead. In the three months remaining,
Humphrey used his enormous energy to attempt to re-
unite the party and, in the end, he almost did so.

But it was too late. Richard Nixon had been elected by
a whisker-thin margin.

The election of Richard Nixon began a new era in the
story of America in Vietnam. The Johnson Administra-

tion had seemed close to deciding that Vietnam was not the place to fight the war that was being fought. As early as March of 1968, the last Johnson Secretary of Defense, Clark Clifford, had suggested that American troops be withdrawn. The new administration was to adopt a policy of Vietnamization—turning the war over to the Vietnamese. But before that new policy could begin, an event that had taken place in March of 1968 came to light. It happened in the small village that was called, on American maps, My Lai (4).

On March 16, 1968, soliders of the First Battalion of Twentieth Infantry entered the hamlet of My Lai, rounded up the old men, women and children and killed them. The soldiers were not being fired on nor was there any apparent danger from the people of the hamlet.

There was reason to believe that My Lai was a head-quarters for NLF forces, and the Americans had been having a great deal of trouble lately from that area. But nothing in the rules of war permitted what happened on that day. A report was filed with the Army by Lt. Colonel Frank A. Barker. He claimed that 128 enemy troops were killed and that, among other things, three enemy rifles had been taken. He did not explain how one counts over a hundred dead soldiers and only three rifles, nor did he mention the hundreds of civilian dead. In fact, no one mentioned that fact officially, though over one hundred American troops were in the hamlet.

In fact, it was not until one year after the event that Ronald Ridenhour wrote letters to the army and to his congressmen demanding an investigation. Ridenhour had not been at My Lai, but he knew several people who had been, and these friends told the story to him separately.

Under pressure from Ridenhour's congressman, Morris Udall of Arizona, the army began a quiet and slow investigation. Months passed, and many of the people involved were due to be released from the army. After that release, they would be safe from criminal charges for the event. But the story did not remain quiet. Seymour Hersh, a reporter for *The New York Times*, was told about the story by a source in the army and in November of 1969, he ran a full account of the events in that newspaper. Several officers and enlisted men were charged.

The news of the massacre was one more shock to the nation, but in some ways this shock was quite different. By the time that Hersh broke the story, protest against the war had reached new levels. A quarter of a million Americans had marched on Washington that same month. Doubts about the war and the government had become very strong. The official response to My Lai did little to end these doubts. In the end, only Lieutenant William Calley was convicted of serious charges. His jury consisted of officers, most of whom had served in Vietnam. They found his conduct criminal, but at each level of authority above them, including the president, the sentence given to Calley was reduced. In the end he served his brief time in an apartment at a military base.

Calley, a convicted murderer, became a hero to some people. They saw his acts, and those of his colleagues, as a part of war and Calley as a victim of a system that did not understand what he had been through. Others saw him as a scapegoat, a lamb sent to slaughter while the higher officers, who had either ordered the massacre or had failed to report it, escaped conviction. There is more basis for that view than the view of Calley as a hero, for there is nothing to indicate that Calley was other than a willing participant in the murders.

Calley and My Lai presented a strange dilemma. Here was a war in which the enemy looked and dressed just like the rest of the people. Here was a war in which a child might well be carrying a hand grenade. Here was a war in which the deaths of a hundred civilians caused a major scandal and in which it was barely noticed that tens of thousands of civilians (Secretary McNamara estimated one hundred eighty-two thousand) were killed by bombs dropped by invisible planes flying miles above their invisible targets. Right and wrong were not black and white in this war; they were similar shades of gray.

The American people, whether they felt that Calley had been done an injustice or not, were not in support of the slaughter of civilians as a normal part of war. A war in which more than a hundred Americans could have known of such an event and said nothing was not the kind of war that the American public was likely to support for long.

The war was doing something wrong to America. It was dividing its people and killing its young and these young were engaged in killing of their own. My Lai did not end the war in Vietnam. But it was one of the events of 1968 that led to an end to support for the war. To fight a war in a democracy you must have the consent of the people. Americans were withdrawing their consent as much because they disagreed with what the war was doing to America as because they disagreed with the war itself.

Above: The air war came with America's involvement and had many aspects. Here a U.S. jet, flying a reconnaissance mission, casts its shadow over a North Vietnamese facility.

Below: The B-52 Stratofortress bomber was used in operations Linebacker II and Rolling Thunder. Each of the bombs seen here weighs 750 pounds. This photo of one plane on one mission shows nine tons of explosives.

The results of U.S. bombing can be seen in these two pictures. In the upper photo, living quarters are damaged or destroyed. In the lower photo, a railroad line has been put out of service by two "smart" bombs, electronically guided and highly accurate.

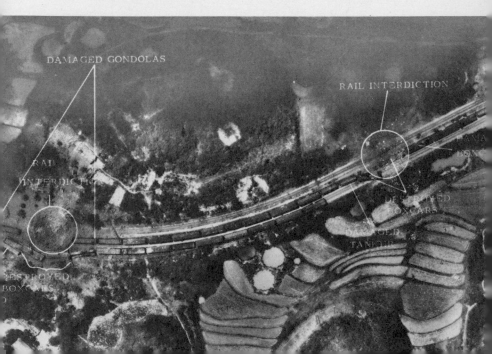

Helicopters played a major role in the Vietnam War. Here one helicopter (upper photo) brings in supplies to troops under attack, while another (lower photo) carries troops on a combat mission.

BURIED POL
KINH KHE, NORTH VIETNAM
20-45N 106-31E
11 JUNE 1966

PERSONNEL

PERSONNEL

BURIED TANK

Above: In an effort to reduce the damage caused by the American bombing, the North Vietnamese built fuel tanks and other facilities underground.

Below: Not all Americans who flew missions over North Vietnam returned safely. Hundreds were shot down and captured. This picture shows a model of a prisoner of war compound. Some Americans spent up to seven years in captivity.

ELEVEN

Talking Peace

Shortly after President Johnson's withdrawal from the 1968 elections and the bombing halt, all sides agreed to meet in Paris to begin talks about ending the war. No one seemed to be in any great hurry to start though. For seven months they debated what shape the table would be. Were the North Vietnamese and the South Vietnamese to be treated as equals and would they face each other across the table? Would the North Vietnamese-sponsored Provisional Revolutionary Government have full participation in the talks? Who would speak first and who would respond to the first speech?

There is a certain craziness about such things being debated while tens of thousands died. But one theory of negotiation holds that such debates on side issues are very important. They allow the parties to test each other and to move around for position on issues that are not at the heart of the debate, on matters that are not the real cause of differences among the parties. The theory holds that these little matters are easier to solve than the real issues and that once they have been solved, the parties know each other well enough, and their strengths and weaknesses are clear enough, to make it easier to find answers to the real and passionate issues.

This is a fine theory and it may even be true, but it looked ridiculous to the watching world, and it gave no basis for any hope that the talks would produce a just and lasting peace.

In this chapter we will be looking in now and then on those negotiations in Paris. We will move from there to events in Vietnam, because the negotiations affected the war and the war affected the negotiations. Neither event took place or could have taken place in isolation from the other. That may seem clear or it may not. It is a tricky point that becomes clearer when you realize that the peace talks were what the war was all about. It is fair to say that because of the way in which the United States fought in Southeast Asia, it could never gain a military victory. Such a victory was possible only through the use of many times more troops than the American political situation would allow—or through invasion of North Vietnam.

It is even truer to say that North Vietnam could not win a military victory in South Vietnam. In the period of American involvement, the North Vietnamese never even won a major battle. The odds in a battle for Saigon, of their beating five hundred thousand American troops plus many more South Vietnamese troops, with the Americans controlling the air, were ridiculously low.

The war was a tie. It probably was always a tie, but it took several years and many lives before that concept was clear to all parties. That is not unusual either. World War I was a tie for most of its course. Thousands of troops died in trenches over gains and losses of but a few square miles of territory. The tie in World War I was broken when millions of American troops joined the battle and tipped the scales.

What do you do if you are in a war and nobody is winning or nobody can win? You have two choices. You can keep fighting until the other side is economically destroyed and can no longer afford to fight, or you can talk peace.

The possibility of economic defeat for either side was very low. The North Vietnamese economy was simple, and its needs were few. In addition, the supply lines to China and Russia were open, and those nations had enough wealth to avoid an economic defeat. The United States could keep on fighting for many years if cost were the only question. The Vietnam War was expensive to America, but the American economy was at its peak during the war years, and the war was not going to disrupt the economic life of the average American.

Since the tie was there, the peace talks had to take place. War is one means of gaining national goals. Talking is another. If the parties could not achieve what they wanted through war, they would try to achieve their same goals through discussion. The purpose of the talks was to attempt to solve politically those problems that were being fought over on the battlefield.

But political discussions are very different from military wars. In war fought to the end, like World War II or the American Civil War, someone wins and someone loses. After the victory, the victor may decide to keep the defeated territory or it may do something else. For instance, it may take its wealth or it may make it a colony or it may require it to sign a very favorable trade treaty. But the choice is its, and the losing nation has very little say in the matter.

Peace discussions between two nations caught in a stalemated war (or a war whose outcome neither side is certain of) are a different matter. Deep inside, both sides know that they are not going to win. Neither one would be the first to say that, of course. If you admitted that you could not win at the bargaining table and the other side insisted that it could, what on earth would there be to talk about?

Neither side, then, will admit that the war is stalemated. Both sides pretend that they are winning, but both sides know that both they and the other side are lying. There is a great deal of what is sometimes called posturing. Each side will try to look as strong and as forceful as possible.

At the end, though, there will not be a clear winner and a clear loser. Both sides will have gained some of their goals and neither side will have gained everything.

Each side brings into the discussions a set of goals it wishes to gain. At first they ask for as much as they would hope to gain by a military victory. When both sides do this, they start out with one saying, "Give me everything I want," and the other side saying the same thing.

The Paris peace talks were more difficult then normal because there were four parties in them with at least three different goals. The Americans looked at the talks as a way of ending their involvement in the war without looking as if they had abandoned a friend. So a key American objective was a cease-fire followed by withdrawal of foreign troops (American and North Vietnamese). The North Vietnamese, the NLF, and the South Vietnamese were more concerned with what happened after the fighting had ended. They had opposing views on the political parts of the talks.

What political decisions would be reached at the talks? Would North Vietnam recognize the government in Saigon? Would they, instead, demand a common election to end the national division, or would they accept a free and open election in South Vietnam in the hope that their southern allies would win and the two nations would gradually be joined?

The Americans wanted peace first. After that, they felt that the political questions could be worked out one way or another. The Vietnamese wanted the political questions answered before they would agree to stop fighting. There was a stalemate at the conference table as well as on the battlefield.

In January of 1969, Richard Nixon became the president of the United States. Shortly after he took office, the North Vietnamese carried out attacks on dozens of

South Vietnamese towns much like the Tet offensive a year earlier. More than a thousand Americans were killed in those attacks, and Nixon responded strongly.

He ordered Operation Menu to begin. This involved the bombing of North Vietnamese military targets located in Cambodia. It was believed that the North Vietnamese had one or more secret command posts located near the Cambodia-Vietnam border, and it was hoped that if these were wiped out, the military efforts from the north would weaken. The bombing lasted fourteen months and included 3,650 B-52 raids. It was done entirely in secret.

The raids were probably legal. The North Vietnamese were using Cambodia as a base for war against South Vietnam. The Cambodian government had given some permission to bomb in the area. So why were the raids kept quiet?

There are two reasons. First, the idea that Nixon wished to give the American people was that the war was ending. The raids in Cambodia would have given the opposite idea. Second, the American people had never been asked to commit themselves to this war. There had been no declaration of war. There had been no work done to show that this was America against North Vietnam. From Kennedy, through Johnson, to Nixon, the presidents had all wanted to avoid making a big deal about Vietnam. This approach was all right before 1965, but by that year, and certainly by 1969, America was deep into the war, and everybody knew it. Still, though, no one wanted to say it out loud. Letting everyone know that Cambodia was being bombed would have been an announcement that the war was here to stay for a while. So it was kept a secret.

Secrecy is not itself wrong. War cannot always be fought in public nor announced in press releases. But in an open society like the United States, presidents who hide their actions take a grave risk—that of losing the trust of the people. That trust had already been partly lost in regard to Vietnam, and when the Cambodian bombing was made public, very little faith was left.

As the bombing continued, another event took place, which was to confuse and anger the average American. In May of 1969, while the Vietnamization policy was being carried out, two thousand eight hundred American troops were ordered to take hill number 837, better known as Hamburger Hill. The hill was strongly defended. The Americans made eleven separate attacks on it, aided by a million pounds of bombs and one hundred fifty thousand pounds of fiery napalm. When the hill was finally taken, each side had lost five hundred men. The morning after the victory, the American troops were ordered to withdraw.

Some military basis can be found for these losses as with the earlier battle at Khe Sanh. The enemy suffered heavy casualties and a large number of its troops were tied up for a long period of time. Moreover, the NLF had a major military defeat that the whole world saw. But this was the war America was leaving and few Americans saw the sense in five hundred deaths for some unclear purpose in a war that was supposed to be ending.

Two months later, in July of 1969, the first American cutback in troops began. By the end of the year, the

American commitment had been reduced by sixty thousand troops. In August, Ho Chi Minh and Richard Nixon agreed to private and secret peace talks between their two nations in Paris. Le Duc Tho represented North Vietnam and Nixon's National Security Advisor (and later Secretary of State), Henry Kissinger, represented the United States.

The talks were the result of Nixon's use of the carrot and the stick. The "carrot" was the pullback of American forces. The "stick" included the Cambodian bombing and Nixon's message to Ho that some movement toward a settlement was needed to avoid "measures of great consequence and force."

On September 3, 1969, Ho Chi Minh died in Hanoi. Two-thirds of his seventy-nine years had been spent in trying to free his country from foreign control and then to unite its parts. Whether those were his only goals we will never know, though what happened after the end of the war suggest that the ancient Vietnamese hope of ruling all of Indochina was still alive. But we shall see more of that a little later on.

Ho died at the very moment when one could begin to see an end to the war that was the center of his life. In response to the American withdrawals, North Vietnamese activity in South Vietnam slowed a great deal. In 1968, there had been fourteen thousand five hundred Americans killed in Vietnam. In 1969, the number dropped to nine thousand four hundred.

In fact, the ground military action, except for a couple of major incidents, remained very quiet until 1972.

The most important of the incidents took place on

April 29, 1970. Earlier that year, the head of the Cambodian government, Prince Sihanouk, was overthrown by General Lon Nol. Lon Nol was much more concerned than Sihanouk had been about the presence of North Vietnamese military bases along his country's border with Vietnam. That concern grew as American bombing drove the North Vietnamese farther from the border and deeper into Cambodian territory. The United States was giving Lon Nol hundreds of millions of dollars in aid to help him resist the North Vietnamese.

At the end of April, though, the United States took matters into its own hands. Fifteen thousand United States and five thousand South Vietnamese troops invaded Cambodia in what was officially described as an "incursion"—a temporary attack. The object, like that of the earlier bombing was to find and destroy the North Vietnamese central headquarters in Cambodia. There was no such base. The North Vietnamese had no Pentagon, but rather a group of small headquarters that were regularly moved.

The attack was useless, but it had very powerful results. Lon Nol denounced the invasion (though he may have been playing to the crowd). More importantly, there was a tremendous outcry in the United States.

Demonstrations against the move broke out on college campuses all over the United States. Some four hundred colleges were shut down by students for some period of time. One of those colleges was Kent State University in Ohio. The Governor of Ohio called up the National Guard to avoid possible rioting and a group of young and untrained Guardsmen came to the campus. When they saw a large number of students heading in their direction, someone opened fire. The first shot set off a chain reaction, and when the shooting stopped, four students lay dead on the campus lawns with several others wounded.

The response on campuses and throughout the nation was much greater than all earlier protests. The war had come home in a deadly fashion. The Democratic-controlled Congress reacted to these events by repealing the Gulf of Tonkin resolution and barring additional American military activity in Cambodia.

But, as we know, the war in Vietnam had grown increasingly quiet. By the middle of 1970, the South Vietnamese government made a fair claim that more than ninety percent of the villages were under its control. President Thieu had begun what seemed to be a serious land redistribution program and President Nixon announced the withdrawal of one hundred fifty thousand more American soldiers.

The year 1971 began with another extension of the war, though. South Vietnamese troops moved into Laos, where they were quickly beaten back. Again there was strong reaction. Bombs were set off in the United States Capitol and Congressional Democrats voted to support an end to American involvement in Vietnam.

These moves into Laos and Cambodia were meant to put pressure on the North Vietnamese to come to a settlement in Paris. Kissinger had secretly gone to Paris many times and the talks continued, but there were no signs of progress other than the quiet on the battlefields. While the American public seemed to have turned against the war, Nixon and Kissinger seemed not to care about public opinion. They had an idea of how the war should end, and they were prepared to hold out against popular feeling.

The tide of public opinion turned even more against the war in the summer of 1971. Dr. Daniel Ellsberg had been a Defense Department official who was one of a group former Secretary McNamara had asked to put together a history of American fighting in Vietnam. The documents assembled by this group were not shocking in themselves, but read together, they provided evidence that the American involvement in Vietnam had included a lot of lying and failure.

Ellsberg had made copies of the documents and given them to several newspapers. The Nixon Administration tried to stop the printing of what became known as "The Pentagon Papers," but the Supreme Court ruled that the newspapers were free to publish them. One strange result of the Pentagon Papers episode was that some government officials ordered a burglary of the office of Ellsberg's psychiatrist in the hopes of finding something to embarrass him. That crime and the attempt to cover it up became a key factor in the "Watergate" investigations, which were to lead to Nixon's resignation as president.

Still the secret talks went on. At first, the quiet in Vietnam continued. Neither side wanted to end the talks by using much force while the discussions seemed to be moving. To do so would have set the negotiations back many years. By the beginning of 1972, though, there were other factors involved. First, the talks seemed to have reached an important stage. Both sides had invested too much in them to quit now. Second, it was a presidential election year, and President Nixon could not go into the election without some strong signs of progress.

Early in 1972, Nixon informed the nation that the secret talks had been going on for more than two years and that Henry Kissinger had made some fifteen trips to Paris in secret. He also announced that the number of American troops would be reduced to seventy thousand.

What Nixon did not reveal was his strategy in the talks. Nixon had a history of over twenty-five years in public life that showed him to be a bitter foe of communism. Kissinger went to Paris with the message that Nixon was a madman; that he could let loose the nuclear monster at any moment. Kissinger presented himself as the reasonable man trying to create a compromise between his crazed leader and the North Vietnamese. (Kissinger won a Nobel Prize for this role; an Oscar would have been just as correct.)

As time went by, the details of a cease-fire were settled and the parties' attention turned to the harder political issues. North Vietnam had a very strong bargaining chip—hundreds of American prisoners of war. The one factor that could rally the American people was these captive warriors. In the spring of 1972 they sought to gain another chip, that of land. More than one hundred thousand North Vietnamese troops moved suddenly into South Vietnam in March, ending more than two years of battlefront quiet. Nixon was fully prepared for this move. He responded by ordering bombing near Hanoi itself and the mining of Haiphong harbor—the chief northern supply port.

These efforts had a significant effect. The North Vietnamese announced their willingness to accept a cease-fire in place. That is, they agreed to halt the fighting then and there and work out most political issues later. The United States had taken the war to the north in a new and terrifying fashion. The North Vietnamese seemed to accept the idea that American military strength could cause them more harm than talking could.

Those discussions continued into the fall, and the United States and the North Vietnamese reached a basic understanding. However, the South Vietnamese refused to accept the concept of a cease-fire in place. They felt that the North Vietnamese controlled too much territory.

One could see this as silliness or as an act of courage. While American ground troops had largely left Vietnam, it is fair to say that the nation's independence depended on the support of American aircraft in huge numbers. When Thieu rejected the agreement carved out in Paris, he rejected the support of the United States. If that was a matter of great principle, one would have to admire it. However, Thieu's rejection ignored the interests and the wishes of most of his countrymen. His rejection only helped the wealthy aristocrats, who could flee and would flee at the first sign of real defeat. They had nothing to lose until that moment, and at that moment they had the only means of escape—airplanes—in their control. And you can be sure that no farmers would be invited to join them.

It was election time again in America. Nixon was opposed by Senator George McGovern of South Dakota, who had run a campaign based largely on opposition to the war. McGovern had no real chance of being elected, but as the Watergate incidents had established, Nixon did not want to just win the election; he wanted to win big. An end to the Vietnam War would have guaranteed that, because McGovern's one real issue would have disappeared.

Hanoi was a close follower of American opinion. When it was informed that South Vietnam had rejected the proposed treaty, it reacted by announcing that a peace agreement had been reached and would be signed on October 31. It had two reasons for doing so. First, it feared that the whole peace plan was a trick designed to influence the November 7 elections in the United States. It meant to expose that trick. Second, it meant to put pressure on Nixon to keep to the agreements by showing him as the breaker of the pact, knowing that such an image would influence the elections against him.

The efforts to put pressure on Nixon failed. The American answer was delivered by Dr. Kissinger, who announced that peace was at hand. Nixon won reelection by an enormous margin. McGovern carried only Massachusetts and the District of Columbia.

The talks continued, but there seemed to be no hope of an agreement. With Nixon in office for four more years, everybody's plans had changed. Hanoi's position was weak, but it would not admit that. It was a tie again, but a very dangerous one. In order to break the tie, one side had to force the other side to move by some dramatic show of force. The talks collapsed on December 13, 1972, and the show of force was to begin just a few days later.

On December 18, 1972, one hundred twenty-nine B-52s took off from Guam, a Pacific Island thousands of miles from Hanoi. At 7:43 P.M. that night, they arrived over Hanoi and began dropping their bombs. For eleven days they flew in a mission that was named Linebacker II. In that time they dropped one hundred thousand bombs on the cities of Hanoi and Haiphong. Fifteen of these planes were lost during this time and about thirty of their crew members died.

North Vietnamese losses were much greater. The bombs hit one thousand six hundred military buildings, five hundred railroad points, ten airports, and destroyed eighty percent of the electrical power plants in North Vietnam. The number of lives lost was not counted, but it must have been enormous.

The bombing had hit home and had hit hard. It had brought with it outrage as well. The United Nations and the Pope condemned the Christmas bombing.

The North Vietnamese came back to the peace talks as a result. That much is sure, but that was the only gain after so much destruction. When a peace treaty was finally signed on January 23, 1973, North Vietnam got what it wanted—the October terms. The United States had used its most powerful force in its most efficient way and had gained nothing from it at all.

South Vietnamese opposition to the October terms had been overcome by President Nixon's private written statement that the United States would help again if the North Vietnamese attacked. The South Vietnamese had good grounds to accept that personal promise. After all, Nixon had just been reelected in a landslide and had four more years to serve. What they did not know, and few would have guessed, was that in eighteen months Richard Nixon would resign as president, and America's attention would have been turned so far away that Asia would not be noticed again for a long time.

The war in Vietnam had ended, at least as far as America was concerned. In March of 1973, the last of the American troops returned home as did the last of several hundred prisoners held by the North Vietnamese.

For those interested in keeping track of such things, it is not clear as to who had the bad luck of being the last American to die in the Vietnamese War. It is likely though that that death took place far from Southeast Asia in the small town of Johnson City, Texas. For there on the night before the peace was signed, the gigantic and deeply saddened heart of Lyndon Baines Johnson gave out, broken from seeing his dream of a just and great society shattered on a foreign shore.

TWELVE

After the War Was Over

America came home in 1973. Its troops came home. Its prisoners of war came home. Its thoughts came home. America forgot about Vietnam and became gripped with "Watergate." The scandal had begun with what was correctly described as a "third-rate-burglary" of a Democratic Party office during the 1972 presidential campaign. It became a minor scandal when it was learned that persons close to President Nixon had approved the plan, which included the break-in. It became a major scandal when it was learned that persons close to the president had worked to cover up the White House involvement. It became the biggest scandal of the century when it was learned that the president himself had supported the cover-up effort.

Americans had rightly had faith in the strength of their armed forces, the goals for which those forces had been used, and the strength and honesty of their national government. Within a few short years their belief in all three was destroyed.

From almost the moment the Vietnam War ended for Americans, until the late summer of 1974, Watergate captured the nation. In a sense this was an easier problem to deal with, because Vietnam was the first great failure of American arms, while Watergate was one of the great successes of American law. Success is always easier to deal with than failure.

Within a year of becoming vice-president, Gerald Ford was the president of the United States. Richard Nixon's resignation and Ford's skillful handling of the first few months of his presidency had done much to return a feeling of normal life to America. Most Americans, understandably, wanted to forget Watergate and had forgotten Vietnam.

But the war in Vietnam had not ended. In fact, in the eighteen months between the end of American combat in Vietnam and the resignation of Richard Nixon, the peace treaty had collapsed. There were no major campaigns, no Tet offensives, but tens of thousands of Vietnamese had been killed or injured in the regular fighting that continued.

With Nixon's resignation, the North Vietnamese may have felt that the American commitment to South Vietnam had ended. Or they may have needed the two years of relative peace and freedom from constant bombings to build up their strength. Whatever the cause, by

January of 1975, they felt that the time was right to launch a new offensive in South Vietnam.

In that month, three hundred thousand North Vietnamese troops moved down the Ho Chi Minh Trail and quietly assembled in the area of Ban Me Thuout, north of Saigon. That was not where they had been expected to attack. The South Vietnamese had expected that the attack would come from farther north, directly across the Demilitarized Zone. The North Vietnamese had created some activity in that area to support that belief and the South Vietnamese had responded by placing a major part of their troops at Pleiku, some forty miles to the north of Ban Me Thuout. The North Vietnamese troops were between the South Vietnamese Army and the South Vietnamese capital, and nobody knew it.

The North Vietnamese attacked Ban Me Thuout on March 10, 1975. The South Vietnamese were taken by surprise and the city was taken in three days.

President Thieu met with his military advisors at Cam Ranh Bay and decided to bring all of his troops from the northern part of South Vietnam to the provinces surrounding Saigon. This decision was like the one the French had made a century before. If Saigon and the ports in the south could be held, the South Vietnamese could rebuild their strength and hope for American help while holding on to the most important part of their nation.

There was a major difference between the French experience and the South Vietnamese effort though. The troops withdrawn from Pleiku and Hue and other northern areas quickly ran into North Vietnamese and NLF units and even more quickly began to panic. What was to have been a slow and careful retreat ended up as a wild race for safety. Hundreds of thousands of troops rushed down highways that were badly in need of repair. There they were met by an even larger number of civilians also heading for the safety of the south. When the two groups ran into enemy fire, any hope of an orderly and disciplined response to the North Vietnamese attack ended.

Now the North Vietnamese were faced with a problem. They had no idea that they would be as successful as they had been. Their plan called for bringing a large force to South Vietnam, taking some important places, and waiting out the monsoon season. The major attack would come after the monsoon had ended.

Now, though, total victory seemed possible, but such a victory might be expensive. So the North Vietnamese offered a deal. They would agree to a coalition government that would combine, they said, all the many groups in South Vietnamese politics if President Thieu would resign. Thieu refused to do this and the North Vietnamese started the second part of their attack.

Hue fell to the North Vietnamese on March 25. Da Nang was taken on March 30. The huge American-built base at Cam Ranh Bay fell a few days later. The South Vietnamese forces, outnumbered now by three to one, were pushed back to a small area around Saigon. Their final defensive line was centered at Xuan Loc, just thirty-eight miles from the capital city.

In one short month the situation had grown desperate. President Ford asked the Congress to pay for great amounts of military aid. Even if the Congress had been in the mood to do that, the aid would have been far too late in arriving, for the end was already at hand.

The South Vietnamese Army made its best showing of the war at Xuan Loc, holding out against superior forces with no real chance of victory. The battle raged for twelve days, but when defeat came on April 21, the road to Saigon was open. President Thieu resigned and flew out of South Vietnam with what some claim was a small fortune.

The North Vietnamese circled Saigon with thirteen divisions of troops. At this crucial moment there was no leader in Saigon, for when Thieu resigned the remaining officials of the government spent several days arguing about who would take his place. This would almost be funny if it were not so much like the events of the past few years. A debate about who led South Vietnam at that point was like having an argument over who was the captain of the *Titanic* after it hit the iceberg.

The picture of a sinking ship is a good one. The United States had started to bring its diplomats home in March. By mid-April the American airlift included thousands of South Vietnamese who had worked with the government and whose lives were in danger if and when the North Vietnamese captured Saigon. Tens of thousands of others were left behind because Saigon fell very quickly. The formal surrender took place on April 30, 1975, and the nation, for good or evil, was one again.

Strangely, in the same week as the North Vietnamese won their final victory of Saigon, the Cambodian communist forces, the Khmer Rouge, won control of the

Cambodian government. One of the basic ideas that had led the United States into war in Southeast Asia was the concept of monolithic communism. A "monolith" is a large slab of stone. A belief in monolithic communism was a belief in the idea that the communist movement was unified; that one communist held the same basic beliefs and values as any other and operated under one common plan. But the Khmer Rouge were mainly backed by the Chinese communists while the North Vietnamese ended up being backed by the Russians.

The Russians and Chinese had been arguing for years about what form of Communism was the right one. Their rivalry had increased over the years. By 1972, the Chinese had begun to warm toward the United States. This worried the Russians greatly. One result of this Chinese-American relationship was that China slowed down its support of the North Vietnamese, while Russia began to give more and more aid to them. Russia and China had been traditional, historical enemies (just as China and Vietnam had been) and the forces they supported in Vietnam and Cambodia would soon be fighting each other—though both were "communist."

Such combat is often called "proxy" fighting and that idea is an important one to understand in a dangerous world. There are only a few nations in the world that have usable nuclear weapons (that is, both the weapons and a system to use them well—either missiles or very modern airplanes.) If those nations were to come into direct combat against each other, the danger that nuclear weapons would be used would be very great.

At the same time, those nuclear nations are so powerful that they have allies all over the world, even though their contacts with the other nuclear nations are not always friendly. Because nuclear nations cannot fight each other (because of the danger of nuclear war) and because they come into conflict so often, they have relied on proxies (substitutes) to do their fighting for them.

The Korean War was basically a proxy war. The Vietnamese War was certainly one. Smaller military efforts in Africa and Central America can also be described as proxy wars. But all of these were proxy battles between East and West, between communism and the democratic states. What would soon occur between Cambodia and Vietnam was a proxy war between the two communist giants—the Soviet Union and the People's Republic of China. We will see some of that conflict shortly. For the moment though, let us return to Vietnam itself and see what effects the North Vietnamese victory had.

The North Vietnamese at first adopted the theory that there were still two Vietnams, which would only be reunited when the South Vietnamese government (the heirs of the NLF) agreed to do so. That government found it necessary to "reeducate" hundreds of thousands of its citizens. These people were forced into camps in the countryside where they listened to political lectures and did manual labor (including searching for land mines by hand) until they agreed to support the new rulers.

A large, but unknown, number of others were forced to move to the north, where they were never heard from again.

The myth of two Vietnams ended in the summer of 1975. Both countries applied for membership in the United Nations. The United States voted against this and they were not admitted. The North Vietnamese announced that the American action was a violation of the Paris agreement. They did not explain why an invasion of South Vietnam was any less of a violation. Since the agreement was broken, they argued, that part that called for two independent states was no longer in effect.

Ho Chi Minh's dream had come true, though he did not live to see it. Saigon was no longer Saigon, but Ho Chi Minh City. Vietnam was one nation and free from foreign countries. Centuries before, the Vietnamese had struggled to unite their nation, and when they had succeeded, they turned to the west and looked at Cambodia. The Cambodians themselves had launched a series of border raids against Vietnam in the time following the collapse of the Thieu government. They claimed that they were only seeking to get back territory that had been theirs before. The Vietnamese responded by taking the Poulo Wai Islands in the Gulf of Siam, territory that had been ruled by the Cambodians.

The border war with Cambodia was interrupted, though, by trouble at home. The communists had never been more than one major group among the Vietnamese nationalists. Because of their unity and their foreign allies, they had been the strongest. But there were many Vietnamese nationalists who hated the communists as much as they did Diem and Thieu.

Chief among these were the Buddhists, and in 1976, that group began passive resistance to the communist government. Passive resistance means taking peaceful action that disrupts the government. Streets may be blocked, people may refuse to go to work, marches may be made against the government. But the protestors do not use weapons or fight the police. Gandhi used this tactic in India and Martin Luther King did so in the United States.

A number of Buddhist monks and nuns set themselves afire in the streets of Vietnam. Of course, this time there were no television cameras to record the awful scene. Hundreds of thousands of other Vietnamese showed their dissatisfaction by fleeing the country by boat. These were dangerous journeys across the sea in small boats that were overcrowded and likely to be sunk by typhoons. Untold numbers of Vietnamese died in these escape efforts. Many more made it safely to friendly nations, from where they were resettled around the world.

Vietnam was not only troubled by internal dissent, it was also having difficulties with its neighbor to the north —China. As is traditional in communist nations, the Vietnam government was opposed to private businesses. Industry and commerce were to be run by the state. In 1978, the government began a crackdown on private business. In Vietnam, and in many other parts of Asia, private business meant Chinese-run businesses. Over the centuries hundreds of thousands of Chinese had moved to the various parts of the world and had started small colonies and many successful businesses.

When the Vietnamese began to harass the Chinese business population, tensions with China grew and a number of small battles broke out in the border area. In mid-1978 China cut off all aid to Vietnam, and in November of that year the Vietnamese signed a treaty with the Soviet Union. The seeds of a Vietnam-China conflict had been sown again.

On Christmas Day in 1978, one hundred thousand

Vietnamese troops invaded Cambodia in support of the ten thousand-member Kampuchean National United Front for National Salvation. The Khmer Rouge forces were completely defeated. The Vietnamese captured or killed one-half of the Khmer Rouge Army and overthrew the government headed by Pol Pot. On January 11, 1979, the new Republic of Kampuchea was declared.

The Chinese had backed the Khmer Rouge and were greatly concerned that the Vietnamese actions meant a new wave of Russian-Vietnamese imperialism in Asia. To stop this, the Chinese invaded Vietnam in February with one hundred thousand troops, making rapid progress in the north. The Vietnamese gathered their forces and slowed the Chinese attack. The Chinese pulled back after having reached their main goal—letting the Vietnamese know that China would not allow expansion by an Asian state supported by the Soviet Union.

This story then ends where it began. Vietnam was one nation again, under attack by China, and eyeing Cambodia as a potential victim of its own. One expert has described the history of Southeast Asia as a "Turning Wheel." It turns and returns like the monsoons of spring. After each destructive season, a time of rebuilding takes place, only to be followed again by an era of death.

It is as though these peoples were characters locked into a theater, forced to perform the same play over and over hopelessly. Real actors do that all the time, of course. But most plays, like most stories, have a happy ending. In Vietnam, the happy ending has not yet been written.

Bibliography

ANCIENT VIETNAM THROUGH
THE FRENCH COLONIAL PERIOD

These books may deal with other parts of Vietnam's history as well but are good sources for information about the pre-American period.

Buttinger, Joseph, *The Smaller Dragon.* (Praeger, 1958)
Fall, Bernard, *The Two Vietnams.* (Praeger, 1963)
Kalb, Marvin and Abel, Ellie, *Roots of Involvement.* (Norton, 1971)
*Poole, Peter, *Dien Bien Phu, 1954* (Watts, 1972)
Shaplen, Robert, *A Turning Wheel.* (Random House, 1979)

* These books were written for younger readers.

AMERICA IN VIETNAM

——, *The Pentagon Papers*. (Bantam Books, 1971)

Arnett, Peter and Maclear, Michael, *The Ten Thousand Day War*. (St. Martin, 1981)

*Fincher, E. B., *The Vietnam War*. (Watts, 1980)

Fitzgerald, Frances, *Fire in the Lake*. (Random House, 1973)

Halberstam, David, *The Best and the Brightest*. (Random House, 1972)

Harrison, J. P., *The Endless War*. (McGraw-Hill, 1983)

Karnow, Stanley, *Vietnam: A History*. (Viking, 1983)

*Lawson, Don, *The War in Vietnam*. (Watts, 1981)

Podorhetz, Norman, *Why We Were in Vietnam*. (Simon and Schuster, 1983)

Snepp, Frank, *A Decent Interval*. (Random House, 1977)

SPECIALIZED BOOKS

Goff, Stanley, *Brothers: Black Soldiers in Nam*. (Presidio Press, 1982)

Hersh, Seymour, *My Lai Four*. (Random House, 1970)

Hubbell, John, *A Definitive History of the American Prisoner-of-War Experience in Vietnam*. (Readers Digest, 1976)

Marshall, S. L. A., *Vietnam: Three Battles*. (Quality Paperbacks, 1982)

Pisor, Robert, *The End of the Line: The Siege of Khe Sahn*. (Ballantine Books, 1982)

**VanDevanter, Linda, *Home Before Morning*. (Warner Books, 1983)

** This is the only book of this group that is written about a woman's experience in Vietnam.

VIETNAMESE VIEW

Dung, Van Tien, *Our Great Spring Victory*. (Monthly
　　Review, 1977)
Van Canh, Nguyen, *Vietnam under Communism*. (Hoover
　　Institute Press, 1983)

PERSONAL ACCOUNTS

These books tell of individuals experiences in the war. War
is not pleasant and these books contain some very unpleasant
stories.

Baker, Mark, *Nam*. (Morrow, 1981)
Caputo, Philip, *A Rumor of War*. (Ballantine, 1978)
Kovic, Ron, *Born on the Fourth of July*. (Pocket Books,
　　1977)
Santoli, Al, *Everything We Had*. (Random House, 1981)

Two other books are part of a recent effort to look back at
the Vietnam War from a scholar's point of view. These are:

Salisbury, Harrison, ed., *Vietnam Reconsidered*. (Harpers,
　　1984)
Summers, Harry, *On Strategy: A Critical Analysis of the
　　Vietnam War*. (Dell, 1982)

Index

American advisors, 90–91, 92,
  95
American airlift, 161
American support for war,
  126–27, 136, 149, 151
Annam, 7, 8, 11, 27
Annamese Cordillera, 4, 8
Anticommunism in U.S., 45,
  51, 67
Antiwar demonstrations, 106,
  112, 126–27, 135
  in Chicago, 133
  at Kent State, 149–50
Antiwar movement, 123, 132
  roots of, 112–113
Au-Co, 4
Au, Trieu, 7
AWOL rate, 121

Bach Dang, battle of, 8
Ban Me Thout, 159

Barker, Frank, 134
Beau, Paul, 31
Bombing of North Vietnam,
  125, 146
  Christmas, 155
  civilian deaths from, 126,
  146
  cutback in, 131, 141
Bon, Ly, 7
Bonaparte, Napoleon, 17, 20
Bo Tree, 6
Buddha, 6
Buddhist religion, 6–7
Buddhists, 83, 85, 112, 164–65

Calley, William, 135–36
Cambodia, 24, 27, 149, 161–62
  invasion by Vietnam, 164,
  165–66
  secret bombing of, 146–47,
  148

Cambodia, ancient, 8–9, 9–10,
    18–19
Cam Ranh Bay, 159, 160
Casualties, 111, 115, 147, 155
Cease-fire in place, 153
Central Intelligence Agency
    (CIA), 46, 72, 73, 80, 86
    as advisors, 91
    and domino theory, 93
Chiang Kaishek, 44
China, 27, 31, 32, 34, 43, 50
    Ho Chi Minh in, 37
    involvement of, 92, 98
    river route to, 21, 25
    as ruler of Indochina, 4–6,
    7–9, 11
    support to Viet Minh, 58
China-U.S. relations, 162
China-Vietnam relations, 161,
    162, 165, 166
Christianity, 14–15
Chu Yuan-Chang, 11
Clifford, Clark, 134
Cochinchina, 24, 26
Colby, William, 80
Colonial rule, 29–31, 38–41,
    47–53
    guerilla wars of, 49–53
    postwar, 47–49
Commission of Reforms, 39
Communist Party, 37
Constitutionalist Party, 36

Dai, Emperor Bao, 39, 46, 47,
    74
Daley, Richard, 133
Da Nang, 96, 109
Dao, Tran Hung, 10
Declaration of war, 98, 146
Deferments, 118, 119
    end of, 120–21
Democratic Party, 132–33

Democratic Republic of
    Vietnam, 47
Diem government, 77–78, 79
    opposed to Buddhists, 83,
    84–85, 90
    overthrow of, 85–87
Diem, Ngo Dinh, 39, 75, 164
    character of, 73–74
    death of, 86, 100
    powerlessness of, 76–77
    relatives and friends of, 77,
    78
Dien Bien Phu, 58, 59, 60–63,
    127–28
Dinh, Emperor Khai, 35
"Domino theory," 67, 93
Dong Khe, 51
Dong Hoi, 51
Dong, Pham Van, 94–95, 106
Don, Tran Van, 91
Draft, 118–21
    resistance to, 120
Drugs, 122
Duc, Thich Quang, 83–84
Duc, Emperor Tu, 26
Dulles, John Foster, 67, 68,
    69, 72

Eisenhower, Dwight, 63, 77,
    82
Ellsberg, Daniel, 151
Empire of Vietnam, 19–20,
    23–24, 27

de Faria, Antonio, 12
Ford, Gerald, 158, 160
Fragging, 122
"Free travel" period, 75
French expansion, 20, 21–23,
    24–28
French interests, 15–16, 21, 75
Fulbright, William, 106

de Galard, Genevieve, 63, 64
da Gama, Vasco, 11
Gandhi, 164
Garnier, Francois, 25
De Gaulle, Charles, 82
Geneva agreements, 69–70,
    74–75, 79, 93
    U.S. refusal to sign, 76
Geneva Conference, 62, 65–70
Giao Chi, 4, 7
Giap, Vo Nguyen, 49, 50, 51,
    52, 60–63
Goldwater, Barry, 93
Green Berets, 115, 116
Gruening, Ernest, 99
Guerilla warfare, 23, 49–50
Gulf of Tonkin incident,
    96–98
Gulf of Tonkin Resolution,
    99–100, 106, 150

Hamburger Hill, 147
Hersh, Seymour, 134
Ho Chi Minh City, 9, 164
Ho Chi Minh Trail, 125–26,
    159
Hue, 4, 12, 159, 160
Humphrey, Hubert, 132, 133

Indochina, 3, 42
Indochinese Communist
    Party, 38
Indochinese Union, 27
International Control
    Commission, 69, 79, 93

Japan, 33, 39–41, 44, 45–46
Johnson administration,
    97–100, 108–10, 113, 126,
    133–34
    and Tonkin, 97–100
Johnson, Lyndon, 84, 88–89,
    92, 105–06, 146

death of, 156
election of, 93, 100, 105,
    107
ends candidacy, 131, 141
and Great Society, 113
and Seaborn mission, 93–95

Kampuchean National
    United Front for
    National Salvation, 166
Kennedy, John, 53, 63 81–82,
    88, 146
death of, 87
and Diem, 84, 86
Kennedy, Robert, 106, 130–
    31, 132
Khan, General, 93, 106
Khe Sanh, 127–28, 129–30, 147
Khmer Rouge, 161, 162, 166
Kingdom of Champa, 8, 12
King, Martin Luther, 131, 165
riots after death of, 131–32
Kissinger, Henry, 148,
    150–51, 152, 155
Kuomintang, 34
Ky, Nguyen Cao, 107

Lac-Long-Quan, 4
Lansdale, Edward, 72–74,
    75–77, 78, 80
Laos, 3, 8, 27, 91, 150
Laotian border, 58, 125, 126
Le dynasty, 11, 12, 13–14, 15
Le Paria, 37
Lodge, Henry, 84, 89
Long, Cia, 17, 18, 19
Louis Napoleon, 21

Magsaysay, Ramon, 73–74
Mandarin system, 17, 18, 27
Mao Zedong, 44
McCarthy, Eugene, 130, 132
McGovern, George, 153–54

McNamara, Robert, 91, 95–96
111, 136, 151
    resignation of, 126
    and Tonkin, 99–100
"McNamara's Fence," 126,
    127
Mekong River, 25, 27
Mekong River delta, 4, 8, 9,
    14, 22, 23
Minh, General, 86, 91, 106
Minh, Ho Chi, 36, 40, 69, 76,
    78, 79, 164
    in China, 37–38
    U.S. support of, 44–45,
        46–47
    as communist, 43–44
    compared to Diem, 74
    death of, 148
Missionaries, 14–15, 24, 25
    political activities of, 19,
        20, 21
    and Nguyens, 16–17
Mongol expansion, 10–11
Monolith, defined, 162
Monsoons, 22
Morse, Wayne, 99
My Lai, 134–36

Nationalist movements,
    31–32, 34–35, 39, 40, 43
    of Ho Chi Minh, 37–38
National Liberation Army,
    46–47
National Liberation Front
    (NLF), 80, 91, 110, 113,
    134, 147, 159
    formation of, 89–90
    at peace talks, 145
    supported by North, 90,
        94, 95
NLF offensives, 91, 106–07,
    108

National People's Party, 34
Navarre, Henri, 58, 59
The New York Times, 130,
    135
Neutralist solution, 91–92
Ngo-Quyan, 8
Nguyen family, 12, 13, 14,
    15, 16–17
Nhu, Madame, 84
Nhu, Ngo Dinh, 78
"Nirvana," 7
Nixon administration, 146–47,
    148–49, 150–51, 155
Nixon, Richard, 63, 95, 117,
    145–46, 152
    election of, 132, 133–34
    and public opinion, 150–51
    race with Kennedy, 84, 88
    re-election of, 153–54,
        155–56
    resignation of, 151, 158

Nol, Lon, 149
Nolting, Frederick, 84
North Vietnamese, supported
    by Russians, 162
North Vietnamese Army, 80,
    108
North Vietnamese offensives,
    145–46, 158–61

Office of Strategic Services,
    46
Ohio National Guard, 149–50
Operation Menu, 146
Operation Rolling Thunder,
    105, 108–09
Operation 34–A, 96–97, 98

Paris peace talks, 141–44,
    151–52

October terms, 153, 154, 155
parties in, 145
secret, 148, 150, 152
Paris peace treaty, 158, 164
Patti, Archimedes, 46, 73
"The Pentagon Papers," 151
Philippines, 3, 31, 72–73
Pleiku, 159
Portuguese, 11–12, 13
Pot, Pol, 166
Potsdam Conference, 46
Prisoners of war, 152, 156, 157
Protectorate, 24
Provisional Revolutionary Government, 141
Proxy wars, 162–63

"Quicksand war," 52

Red Cross, 65
Red River valley, 3, 12, 25
Republic of Cochinchina, 49–50
Revolutionary Youth League, 37
Ridenhour, Ronald, 134–35
Rivière, Henri, 26
Roosevelt, Franklin, 45, 88 89
Rusk, Dean, 99
Russia, 33–34, 37, 43, 98
and North Vietnam, 162, 163, 165, 166

Saigon, 22, 23, 159, 161
Seaborn, Blair, 93–95, 105–06
Seaborn mission, 93–95, 98
Selective Service System, 118–120
Sihanouk, Norodom, 149
Socialist Party, 37

South East Asia Treaty Organization (SEATO), 76, 79, 109
South Vietnamese army, 76 78, 143, 159, 161
panics in retreat, 159–60
South Vietnamese governments, 90, 93, 106
see also Diem government; Thieu government
South Vietnamese navy, 90, 91
Strategic hamlet program, 80–81
Sun Yat-sen, 34

T'ang Dynasty, 7
Taylor, Maxwell, 109
Tay Son brothers, 14, 16
Television coverage, 128–29
Tet offensive, 128–30, 131, 146, 158
Thailand, 3, 24
Thieu government, 150
at peace talks, 145, 153, 154, 155
Thieu, Nguyen Van, 107, 159
resignation of, 160, 161, 164
Tho, Le Duc, 148
Ton, Emperor Duy, 35
Tourane, 22, 23
Treaty of Protectorate, 26
Thrinh family, 12–13, 14, 15, 17
Trung sisters, 5
Tu, Ly Phat, 7
Tunnels, 63

Udall, Mörris, 134
United National Front, 47
United Nations, 50, 163–64
U.S. Capitol, 150

U.S. embassy, 129
U.S. Congress, 98, 99, 100,
    160–61
U.S. Marines, 109
U.S.S. *C. Turner Joy*, 97
U.S.S. *Maddox*, 96, 97
U.S. Senate, 88, 99
U.S. State Department, 66–69,
    75, 85, 94, 107
U.S. Supreme Court, 151
U.S. troops, 114, 117, 118,
    119, 121
  in combat, 110–11, 117
  morale of, 117, 121, 122–23
  numbers, 109, 110, 113–14,
    130
  officers, 118
University of California in
    Berkeley, 106

Vichy government, 40–41
Viet Cong, 79, 80
Viet Minh, 42, 43, 44, 46
  and China, 58
  at Dien Bien Phu, 60–63
  potential victors in
    elections, 65, 66, 69

Vietnam-China conflict,
    165–66
Viet Nam Doc Lap Dong
    Minh, 41
Vietnamese in France, 34–35,
    36–37
Vietnamization, 117, 134, 147
Vietnam Quoc Dan Dong
    (VNQDD), 38
Vietnam, united, 163–65
Vietnam War as tie, 144
Vietnam War songs and
    books, 115–16
Viet people, 4, 5, 8–10
Village chiefs, 78, 80, 90
Villages, 5, 7, 13–14, 18
  as political center, 32, 78

Watergate, 151, 157–58
Westmoreland, William, 111,
    130

Xuan Loc, 160, 161
Xuan, Ly, 7

Yuan Dynasty, 10